The Recovering Politician's
Twelve Step Program to Survive Crisis

Jonathan Miller, Editor

TABLE OF CONTENTS

EDITOR'S NOTE

By Jonathan Miller, former Kentucky State Treasurer

Hi, I'm Jonathan. And I'm a recovering politician.

In fact, since I left politics after serving two terms as Kentucky's elected State Treasurer, I founded and currently publish a Web site called…you guessed it…*The Recovering Politician*. With the contributions of a few dozen former politicians – and other experts who've made recent career or life transitions – we offer an insider analysis of today's scandals and crises, as well as tomorrow's second acts.

Be sure to join us at *TheRecoveringPolitician.com,* sign up for our free weekly newsletter, and check out our online TV show that offers a timely, insiders' look at the nation's most high-profile scandals and crises, with our expert advice and analysis.

One important disclosure about the book title and my self-penned moniker: I do not belong to a traditional twelve step program. But as a great admirer of friends who have battled real addictions, and a proud advocate of programs that empower them, I have learned that many of the same principles espoused in recovery – candor, humility, compassion – can be a valuable tonic for those whose addictions to power, attention, control and the limelight may have placed them in a position of crisis.

So while some references to the language of recovery might elicit a few chuckles, I compiled this book with solemn respect for those who have bravely joined twelve step programs to better themselves, as well as for those who have developed these curricula and saved so many lives in the process.

The use of recovery terms also reveals another particular passion of mine: To prove F. Scott Fitzgerald wrong – that there are meaningful and fulfilling second (and third…) acts in American life. You may have run across this book because you are currently suffering through a difficult crisis – in your firm, career or family. You likely know of a close friend, relative or business associate who has had to endure a challenging or embarrassing public episode.

If my co-authors and I accomplish anything, it is to empower you, through the sharing of our own experiences, with the comfort of knowing that recovery and rehabilitation are always around the corner; and that your journey, no matter how difficult it might seem in the present moment, will provide invaluable lessons for your own next act. We hope that some of the lessons we learned from our own crises – as discussed in the following chapters – can be helpful to you as well.

FOREWORD

By Artur Davis, former U.S.
Congressman from Alabama

It may be helpful to begin by describing what this book is not: The pages to follow are not an updated primer on how to win friends or influence people, or a survey on how to hone the talent of persuasion. Nor is this a series of ruminations on the art of wielding power. Therefore, it may be uninspiring to readers who subscribe to the theory that the arc of success is rooted in some combination of intuitive or developed brilliance.

But the men and women who wrote these chapters know better. Each of us has lived first-hand the axiom that "if you wish to make God laugh tell Him your plans." This book's abiding premise is that the vagaries and friction of life will alter even the trajectory of a genius, much less us mortals; and it will typically do so in the form of an unanticipated crisis. That crisis may take the form of a searing, blinding moment of failure; or more conventionally, it may be a critical mass of bad news that built over time. It may be the product of what one's own humanly flawed judgment has done to him, or it may be the classically unfair much ado about nothing.

Most of the time, this crisis will begin in the form of a disclosure, one that keeps unfolding in an incomplete but corrosive way. The hydraulic pressures of modern communication mean that the unfurling of additional revelations may come in different media venues, with varying levels of credibility, and that there will be no one point when every knowable element is lined up on the same page at the same time.

There are no Supermen theories here and not much patience for the notion that events are but a crescendo of unstoppable historical tides. We already know that crises happen to the worthy and unworthy alike. The authors will argue that there are reasons beyond luck and cosmic favor why some crises are handled more skillfully than others. There are strategic tools that are worth deploying, hard lessons to be derived from past successes and failures.

Above all, the logic of the authors is that this thing called crisis management (or if you prefer "reputation" management, because that is the commodity really at risk) is descriptively a very prime ingredient in who has made it and who hasn't. If you doubt that, by the way, some ready facts are in order. It is not a cynical statement, but a recitation of recent history, to note that the last four Presidents each came reasonably close to ending up in a political dustbin. The prototype is Bill Clinton in the winter of 1992, navigating dual charges that he engaged in an extramarital affair and that he had manipulated his network in Arkansas to escape a draft notice.

Already less remembered is the near implosion of Barack Obama when video surfaced capturing incendiary racial and anti-American rhetoric from the pastor of his own church. Receding from memory is the last weekend of George W. Bush's campaign in 2000, when a news report revealed that Bush's past drinking troubles had led him to a DUI citation as a young man. And all but disappeared is the slow burn over George H.W. Bush's alleged ties to the web of covert activity by government operatives that traded arms to the reviled Ayatollah Khomeini's Iranian regime and financed right wing guerillas in Nicaragua.

By the way, the fact that some of these tales are shadowy or forgotten to all but the most devout news nerds is an exhibit of crisis management working wonders. Of course, a promising New York Congressman named Anthony Weiner, who developed a fondness for engaging online attractive young women on his Twitter feed, famously illustrates the reverse kind of management; the same for an 80s era senator named Gary Hart, whose very viable presidential hopes did not outlast a press stake-out of his townhouse the weekend he had an overnight female visitor.

Now to the specifics of what this book delivers. We will spend a lot of time on the critical role that "narrative" plays. Former Maryland Lt. Gov. Michael Steele (who also chaired a national political party; but then again these pages are scrupulously bi-partisan) discusses just how imperative it is to render an account that is truthful, but necessarily strives to render facts in a sympathetic manner. Steele stresses the reality that as uncomfortable as it is to be in a firestorm, conceding to adversaries or journalists the work of divulging details will usually not end well.

The reader will recognize how much the last two presidential campaigns bear out that insight: On the winning side, Barack Obama's choice to proactively address his relationship with Jeremiah Wright in a seminal speech on the conundrum of race, versus Mitt Romney's crucial failure to spell out what it meant to lead a private equity company to an electorate still reeling from a financial crisis driven by private equity's cousins. The corporate-minded reader will think of the software company Hewlett Packard's public bungling of an internal investigation into supposed misconduct by its CEO. Many readers will think of Penn State University's inability to provide any good context for its failure to expose a child molester in the upper echelon of its football program.

Several of these chapters are admonitions against the vagaries of human nature under distress. Former Missouri State Senator Jeff Smith's account of resorting to lies in the face of impending disaster is a clear-cut explanation of how pressured people react to all manner of disasters; and it evokes Clinton stumbling into his impeachment by not coming clean about Monica Lewinsky. But no less valid is former Kentucky State

Treasurer Jonathan Miller's counsel that there is such a thing as blowing bad news out of proportion with too rapid and undisciplined a response (Anthony Weiner undoubtedly wishes he had not claimed he was hacked, and former Republican presidential candidate Herman Cain could have done without offering his own rendition of just why a particular employee might have thought he was inappropriate with her). Former Suffolk County (NY) Executive Steve Levy tells us that the normal human act of incessantly talking through a dark patch and airing all the laundry to feel cleansed has risks.

Former U.S. Senator Carte Goodwin – who found himself filling the legendary Robert Byrd's shoes during the gap between Byrd's death and a special election to pick his replacement – counsels that humility and a dose of humor are valuable assets in the throes of a crisis, and can provide clarity during the storm. Former Florida legislator Loranne Ausley offers the pointed observation that the ordinary impulse to keep lashing out at the ones who have fought us or wronged us is not only counter-productive to restoring a public image; that path ignores the good work, much less the personal restoration, that can come out of rivals reemerging as collaborators. And Jimmy Dahroug, a former legislative candidate in New York, adds the caveat that – in a book heavy on advice – it is necessary to resist the temptation to surrender to advice at the expense of a personal compass.

Not everything in these pages is the stuff of instant career life or death. The chapters by former Atlanta City Council President Lisa Borders and former Pennsylvania legislator Jennifer Mann remind us that sometimes crisis is borne in policies or actions that have failed, or are struggling to bear results. (Think of the sharply divergent fates of the last two Presidents in defending, respectively, their record in building an economic recovery or prosecuting a war; or Facebook, in restoring its investor base after an unexpectedly soft public stock offering; or Walmart, in assuring regulators that its entanglement with foreign bribes in Mexico is a thing of the past.) Borders writes about the imperative of communicating a plan to reverse and fix damage (a chapter any number of capsized Wall Street entities might have taken to heart in 2008), and Mann makes the underrated, highly valuable point that in the current culture, trouble recurs for companies and politicians. Storing up good will for the inevitable next storm is vital.

So far, the astute reader will notice that this book looks for pathways to avoid or navigate out of disaster. That is fair, but it will be worth dwelling on the journey from alcoholism that former Kentucky Secretary of State John Y. Brown, III describes. Yes, his chapter is valuable on the narrow question of how to handle the point when an unpleasant chapter in one's private life is about to burst into view; but there is substantially more than that. It is stunningly vivid prose (this is a first- class novelist waiting to be born); that reminds us that, more than just shattering images, crises can wreck lives. And those lives have to be not just rehabilitated, but sometimes also reconstructed, along lines never imagined. There is remarkable wisdom here about the awful vantage point from ground zero.

This, by the way, is hardly a collective work of autobiography. But readers will appreciate that some of the most bitingly direct observations to come are drawn from personal experience. Jeff Smith was a political prodigy whose narrow loss of a Democratic primary for Congress seemed only an interlude on a path to stardom. Until his campaign accounts attracted the attention of federal investigators, and until Smith made the error of trying to "spin" a legal crisis by, well, lying. His encounter with the consequences of compounding trouble with deception took guts to relive.

In the same vein, former Oregon legislator Jason Atkinson was quite possibly on the way to the governorship when an accident with a handgun nearly ended his life. In a cruel twist, Atkinson's gubernatorial hopes were undone within weeks of the surgery that saved him. Atkinson bravely recounts in his chapter how his own truthful rendering of what happened still wasn't enough to transcend a crisis of perception that seems the depth of unfairness. Similarly, the former Speaker of the Missouri House, Rod Jetton, writes movingly about the lessons from his own brush with personal scandal and criminal investigations in a chapter on the ownership of mistakes and the necessary role of accepting responsibility in emerging from a cloud. Loranne Ausley's observations about moving on from confrontation are flavored with what she shares about the former rival who helped deliver her premature child.

We do know that there will be criticism that this book gets it right descriptively but misses that crisis management is just some phase of broader excellence; that it is the equivalent is dwelling at length on Lebron James' high shooting percentage in games against other playoff contenders, or Adele's penchant for killing it in live award show performances. Yes, skilled people do a variety of things well. But the astute reader will note that the stories of high performance in these chapters sometimes follow egregiously dumb or bad behavior that made the crisis in the first place. They will also do well to remember that strategic ineptitude on one front, thankfully, leaves space for genius on others. After all, it was the hapless campaign of John McCain that killed in its cradle a potentially mortal story in the nation's leading paper about a possible romantic relationship between McCain and a lobbyist. And the most immensely gifted politician of his generation could have yielded a book twice this length about just how to exacerbate a frivolous lawsuit into an impeachment.

Our work, of course, is vulnerable to the judgment that it leans too heavily toward the political. After all, each one of its chapters is the handiwork of a former candidate and elected official. To be sure, they are sprinkled with observations about the non-political world; and as these chapters were drafted, the media was consumed with the details of a dethroned championship cyclist who told a pack of lies about performance enhancing drugs; a college football star trying to explain that he was the victim and not the author of a weird hoax about a girlfriend who never existed; a multi-Grammy winner putting the best face on an ill-advised choice to lip-synch at an presidential inauguration. Some of that cultural furniture appears in this book and will be mined for lessons. But in the interests of disclosure, the former public servants who wrote these pages will craft a lot more guidance from the world we spent much of our lives occupying. It's not a bad thing.

And as satisfied as we are with the political focus, we emphatically reject the temptation to take this book as an instructional tool solely for the kind of people who live on a high wire, corporate or political, or who have somehow insinuated their way into this thing we call celebrity. The authors of this book would add a strong word of advice about how shortsighted that would be. There is much in these chapters that ought to speak to the mid-level manager who has received the news that his employees are gaming their shifts, and who has to offer a report to his superiors; or the coach who thinks an athlete buffed up too much this summer for all the new muscle to be the product of extra training. It would take a dense reader not to hear the persistent notes in this book about resilience, responsibility, and grace under fire and to miss the universality of those themes.

We also don't put much stock in the inevitable jibe that crisis management advertises a reverence for "spin" and obfuscation. We just disagree. The most profound answer to the charge of excessive cynicism is, in some ways, the poignancy of Jeff Smith's testament about the wages of trusting something other than the truth.

But the equally valid fact is that the writers respect that, for all its power, truth gets outwitted by deception much too often, and the complexity of facts renders them prone to being misunderstood. To know those limitations of our mind and our media, and to craft an approach to overcome them, is not just wise strategy. It is a celebration of a particularly humble and accessible kind of mastery, one that is open to the ones of us who appreciate that saints are just sinners who got back up.

Lastly, a word of acknowledgment: While the name of Jonathan Miller headlines one chapter – a sage reminder on the need to know that a crisis is at hand before entering crisis mode – this book bears his wisdom and touch on every page. It also lives out his animating vision, that a collection of Democrats and Republicans whose last stint on the public stage was in many instances the one we wish we could take back, still have something to offer by way of our accumulated judgments. If this book thrives, or even if it just touches your imagination, it is a triumph of Jonathan's confidence in redemption.

STEP ONE:

Take a Deep Breath...With Your Mouth Shut

By Jonathan Miller, former Kentucky State Treasurer

The worst day of my life opened much like the celebrated final scene of *The Social Network*: A nebbishy Jewish guy, hunched over his laptop, obsessively clicking and re-clicking the refresh button and praying for a small miracle.

Except unlike Facebook founder Mark Zuckerberg's alter ego, I wasn't hunting for lost love.

No, I was the prey.

Early that bitter December morning, I sat anxiously awaiting the online edition of my hometown daily paper. A young reporter, upset by a series of critical posts written about him by a blogger friend of mine, had launched a counter-offensive – against me – interviewing dozens of my colleagues and staffers, sharing gossip through the anonymous netherworlds of the blogosphere, and filing a procession of open records requests for my travel expenses, my phone logs, my email trail.

His objective? To prove – somehow, some way – that I

had been having an extramarital affair with a subordinate.

He never found a smoking gun. He couldn't, after all. Because for all of the stupid, human mistakes I'd made during my first four decades, this just wasn't one of them.

But as the article appeared on my computer screen, my worst fears were realized. In a piece that resembled a modern political ad, the reporter had spliced together a mosaic of out-of-context quotes, misleading excerpts of official documents and numerically incorrect data to imply – strongly – that I had been having an affair.

And I was devastated.

Ever since I was a cloying four-year-old, rattling off the Presidents forward and backwards for my parents' friends, my own sense of self-worth intrinsically remained tethered to tangible public achievement: academic and tennis awards, acceptance into the "right" schools (naturally, I chose Harvard, twice), and ultimately, climbing the rungs of the political world at the earliest age possible. It wasn't the fame I was seeking – I still valued a modicum of privacy – and fortunately, I wasn't desperate to have everyone like me (the curse of so many politicians who jump into the arena seeking universal popularity, only to slowly realize that they've chosen precisely the wrong ballpark, inside of which even the most successful players find at least 33% of the folks in the peanut gallery hating their guts.)

Rather, the precocious, over-achieving child in me still craved to be respected, even esteemed, particularly by those who were least likely to give me that TLC: the political and media establishment, many of whom found me too ambitious, too self-promoting, too much like the school-kid in the front of the class, hand perpetually jutting skyward, so damn desperate to show off for the teacher. (Think a cross between *Election*'s Tracy Flick and *Welcome Back, Kotter*'s Horshack, looking much more like the latter.)

And now, all of it seemed to be crashing on top of me. I would be the subject of ridicule, the butt of Frankfort's toxic obsession with both sex and tearing down those who rise too fast.

The ancient Rabbis suggested public humiliation was akin to death. I had finally understood what they meant.

Having lost a father to cancer and a best friend to a drunk driver, I knew grief. And sitting alone in my dark study, watching the sun rise to welcome the worst day of my life, I experienced that familiar tightening of my chest, the same nausea in the pit of my stomach – that hollowed out, dull ache that made me feel like I had been socked in the solar plexus.

I began immediately to manifest all of the Kubler-Ross stages of grief; although denial and bargaining quickly transitioned into anger, where it metastasized for months.

I was furious at the young reporter, of course; but even angrier with his middle-age editor, who, for months, had refused my entreaties for a full-disclosure hearing, assuring me repeatedly – even the very day before the article was published – that there would be no such tawdry implications; that the paper had concluded I had committed no official improprieties, and that my personal life was my private matter.

Most of all, I was disappointed with myself. Like most successful politicians – like most successful leaders in any profession, I imagine – I'm a registered Type A control-freak. Whenever I find myself in the middle of a crisis, I'm driven instinctively to do something – anything – to outwork, outsmart, and out-strategize my adversaries.

And in this situation, with the personal stakes so high, I had failed. Miserably.

I knew intuitively that it was time for me to act – to take urgent, pinpointed, and exhaustive measures to restore my good name. I'd been trained, after all, in the white-hat arts of "rapid response" as a young staffer for Bill Clinton's first presidential bid – the same campaign in which names like Carville and Begala and Stephanopolous became synonymous with a take-no-prisoners approach to crisis management.

I gathered my closest advisers to help me develop a public relations strategy to salvage my reputation. I proposed that I demand a meeting with the paper's editorial board, or write a scathing op-ed, or perhaps even hold a press conference with my supportive wife.

But when I finally – fortunately – opened my ears, I heard the same, consistent counsel: **Take a deep breath...with your mouth shut**.

In my own self-directed universe, I believed that I was in the grips of a calamitous, existential personal crisis. But my friends reminded me that I was viewing this incident from the center of a shallow political bubble, inside of which Capitol hallway gossip and resentment-soaked blog posts waged highly disproportionate influence.

On the real world's radar screen, the issue hadn't even emerged as a tiny blip. A few media outlets had picked up some of the least-salacious snippets of the story; but for the most part, the sounds of silence permeated the body politic.

A consensus emerged among my advisers: The only way that this crisis spark could enflame into a scandal conflagration was if I provided the oxygen. Stay at your desk, Jonathan: Keep your head down, and your lips sealed.

The most compelling advice came from Bill Cox, a contemporary of my father, who had long been a mentor and friend. Bill reminded me of his own experience running for statewide office: During a televised debate, a fringe opponent had accused him of being the subject of an FBI investigation. Bill denied the charge with full bombast, and threatened a libel suit. His response became the news story for the rest of the campaign, which he came from ahead to lose. Had he taken a deep breath with his mouth shut, Bill Cox might have been one of the Commonwealth's greatest Governors.

So I listened. And I struggled. Every instinct in my body wanted to shout my innocence, to utilize the communications and crisis management skills I had honed for two decades in the arena.

But instead, I remained quiet. And as painful and sleepless as the first few days had been, the crisis soon disappeared. The holidays had intervened; and there were no follow-up pieces, no angry letters to the editor, no scolding editorials. Best yet, one of my worst fears never materialized – that my daughters would be teased by their schoolmates: They never even heard about the whole episode until I told them years later.

I later learned from the editor of the state's largest paper that the press had simply concluded that my story just wasn't newsworthy. As I would also hear from so many of my political allies, he credited my restraint.

I had survived.

* * *

Of course, silence won't solve every crisis. In many cases, after taking that deep breath with your mouth shut, you might conclude that an immediate plan of response and remediation is in order. Indeed, in the following chapters, my fellow recovering politicians will share with you our twelve step program on how to survive crises – from highly publicized and politicized scandals, to smaller, more intimate interpersonal struggles. We outline deliberate, focused and vigorous courses of action and reaction, gleaned from our own experiences – often dramatic, sometimes painful – under the bright lights of the political arena.

But before you leap into action, before you employ the empowerment of the following chapters, make sure to take a little time to pause and reflect. Because, like me, you might run the risk of transforming an uncomfortable, mostly private, matter into a much more incendiary public controversy.

The prototype for self-defeating crisis management overreaction was the Watergate scandal. What began as a "third-rate burglary attempt,"[1] with highly tenuous ties to President Richard Nixon, burgeoned into a presidency-wrecking, impeachment-provoking scandal, due to Nixon's own politically suicidal efforts to micro-manage a damage control effort from the White House. Had Nixon resisted the urge to cover up the involvement of some of his political allies – had he kept silent and focused on being President – he'd be remembered today a lot differently.

From Watergate came the maxim, "The cover-up is often worse than the crime." Unsolicited transparency, however, can be equally as fatal.

Before the mid-1980s, politicians' personal lives were considered mostly off-limits by the establishment press. But when presidential frontrunner Gary Hart incredulously dared the media to investigate rumors of his indiscretions – "Follow me around. I don't care. I'm serious. If anybody wants to put a tail on me, go ahead. They'll be very bored."[2] – he declared open season on his own candidacy, which died soon thereafter of a self-inflicted wound on board a little boat called "Monkey Business."[3]

Nourished by their pound of flesh, the press immediately shifted their attention from sex to drugs. From my fortuitous vantage point as a driver/campus organizer/errand boy for Al Gore's 1988 bid for the White House, I watched his policy-laden campaign ground to a halt, as the candidate cloistered himself with senior staff to prepare a proactive admission of his college and Vietnam marijuana use. His tortured and agonized press conference could have blemished his political career, if not for the scandal being completely defused a few hours later when a primary opponent, Bruce Babbitt, responded causally to a reporter's query: "Sure, I tried marijuana...I was a college student in the sixties!"[4]

* * *

Politicians certainly aren't the only ones tempted to respond prematurely or disproportionately to a rumor or accusation, thereby prolonging or even creating a crisis. Let's face it: No matter how thick-skinned an individual purports to be, none of us likes to be criticized, especially not in a personal manner.

And while the Internet has helped serve to democratize our democracy, it's also opened up a brave new world of opportunities to challenge authority, attack enemies, and avenge personal grudges, often under the cloak of anonymity or false pretense. With the rise of new, micro-targeted social media, as well as online consumer rating services, nearly any person in a job that involves public interaction can find Web content that is critical of his or her business, enterprise or, worst of all, personal character.

What's resulted is a rash of rushing reaction – individuals trying to clear their names by responding to online criticism. In some cases, the responses have transformed Lilliputian controversies into newsworthy crises, opening up a whole new battleground for attack. In others, the means of response – sometimes through the use anonymity or artifice – have created a whole new scandal for the firm and/or the individuals involved.

The examples proliferate with the growth of our new media:

- The CEO of Whole Foods, caught posting anonymous blog comments critical of a smaller adversary, leaves his company vulnerable to antitrust charges when the Federal Trade Commission uses the postings as evidence of potential stock manipulation.[5]

21

- During the midst of a withering media inquiry into his extramarital affairs, golfer Tiger Woods' attorneys win a British court order banning publication of "any pictures or video of him nude or having sex," thereby creating a new story that there might be pictures floating around of Woods nude or having sex.[6]

- A Texas State Representative helps torpedo his own bid for Speaker of the House by lashing out at – and thereby publicly airing – anonymous blog comments about his family life and religious stances.[7]

- The software giant Oracle incurs a public relations backlash for an anonymous campaign of trashing its competitors.[8]

- A Florida Congressman's lawsuit, aspiring to fine and potentially jail a citizen for misrepresenting herself in a little-seen blog entitled MyCongressmanIsNuts.com, generates national attention and ridicule.[9]

- A law professor, who had charges against him dropped for soliciting a prostitute, sees the affair draw broader publicity when he sues a blog that had reported on the scandal – for using a copyrighted photo of him.[10]

- An author's decision to report to the FBI negative reviews of her latest novel subjects her to public ridicule and damages her credibility.[11]

It's advisable, accordingly, to be ever wary of the so-called "Streisand Effect": when an effort to censor or remove something published (usually on the Internet) has the reverse effect of publicizing the information far more broadly. The phenomenon was named after the buttah-voiced diva when, in 2003, her legal efforts to suppress photographs of her beachfront residence on a government-sanctioned web site – intended to document coastal erosion – resulted in public downloads of the pictures to spike from a mere six (including two by Streisand's attorneys), to more than 420,000 in the month after her lawsuit was filed.[12]

The famous and the powerful aren't the only ones who'd be wise to heed the advice of reflection before reaction. It's a lesson I've shared with my teenage daughters who've been hurt by a snide remark at school or a snarky Facebook post. While an immediate and symmetric response is often the natural human impulse when taking offense, turning the other cheek is often the most prudent recipe for de-escalation and self-preservation. (And even my daughters recognize that Taylor Swift's infatuation with writing songs decrying her ex-boyfriends is neither good for her career nor her future love prospects.)

So, of course, here's the platinum, trillion-dollar question:

Where do you draw the line between a provocation that should be ignored, and a truly actionable crisis that merits the launch of a crisis management strategy?

My advice is to surround yourself with people you trust – and in higher-profile cases that could involve financial or criminal liability, an experienced crisis management professional – and address together the following questions:

- **What is the gravity of the matter at hand**? Gauge the seriousness of the issue. A personal insult can be weathered. An existential challenge to your business model is a whole other matter.

- **What is your culpability on the issue?** If you are innocent of the charges, repeating a false accusation might only serve to damage your brand. If you have some criminal, moral, or financial liability, a remediation plan is likely in order. (And in these latter cases, it would be wise to surround yourself with advisers with whom communication is privileged: a spouse, an attorney, a physician, a minister.)

- **Are you too small to flail**? Had I been Governor or a Member of Congress, instead of the outgoing State Treasurer, my public visibility might have been too tempting for the press not to apply additional scrutiny. The bigger the fish – powerful politicians, CEOs, Fortune 500 companies – the more necessary it will be to put a crisis management plan in order.

- **How has your core audience been affected?** If slanderous charges appear only on a Web site that your customers or constituents don't tend to read, then you risk impugning yourself with your core audience by raising the matter publicly. If a commonly accessed metric is implicated – your business' Yelp score, your product's Amazon rating – then a response may be necessary.

- **Who is making the charges**? Ignoring the rants of unpopular bloggers or anonymous Internet commenters will not only serve your business interests well, it is guaranteed to lower your blood pressure by at least 10 points. A credible mainstream media source, or a nasty television ad that's seen by millions, would often merit a crisis management response.

- **How motivated is your antagonist?** Assess the staying power of the critic/journalist/competitive rivals who are leveling the charge against you. If you think their venting bile is a one-shot temper tantrum, it would be counter-productive to further provoke them. If their careers or business successes depend on your downfall, consider the most effective means to thwart them.

- **Does the story have legs**? In the most high profile cases, an immediate response is often necessary. But in the gray area crises, giving the matter a little time to play out might be the most effective strategy. If the crisis dies from its own weight, your patience will be rewarded. If the scandal persists, you'll know it's time to pounce into action.

If upon answering these questions, it's become clear that it's time to implement a crisis management strategy, read on. In the following chapters, former politicos share our own war stories; and from our unique vantage point, we offer eleven more steps to empower you to survive and transcend any crisis.

If instead you've determined that a response would only exacerbate your plight, then it's time to walk away.

I know, I know, that's a whole lot more difficult that it sounds.

I've been there.

It's been more than five years since I weathered my worst day, and there isn't a week that goes by during which I don't feel a tinge of anger or frustration about the events that transpired that winter. The lust for revenge – or perhaps stated more loftily, "the pursuit of personal justice" – is an extraordinarily powerful emotional force that's extremely difficult to resist.

But resist, you must. I'm not preaching on moral grounds here, piously scolding you to be the "bigger person." Rather, surrendering to the circumstances is often essential for the most selfish, self-preserving reasons: By striking back at others – even if you are successful in sharing your misery – you put yourself at tremendous risk of inflaming your own predicament.

Even worse, the temptation to avenge yourself can be both a toxic force on your career or business, as well as an emotionally and physically draining strain on your body. The leaders who are most successful, influential and healthiest (mentally and physically) are usually those best adept at swallowing their pride, resisting the temptation to lash out at their enemies, and brushing aside past grievances.

Understand as well that something that might appear a horrible blow to your life or career might in fact turn out to be a disguised blessing. Whether you believe in God's will, karma, or simply Newtonian action-reaction theory, hard times can often reveal sublime breakthroughs. My own worst day was the first small step on my personal journey toward post-political happiness. Enduring such a painful experience has helped immunize me from the small setbacks, insults and affronts that used to drive me crazy.

And it certainly has helped me exorcise my childhood demons. I won't pretend that my addiction to admiration has been "cured": I still love to write and speak; and more candidly, to be read and heard. Even as I type this sentence, I'm hoping that the reader respects me more, due to my personal admission that I crave respect.

But just like a recovering alcoholic, this recovering politician's recognition of personal disorder forces me constantly to self-evaluate, and to push myself to use every potential public opportunity to try to do something with moral relevance. I've quit politics because I now understand that my innate thirst for recognition can never be slaked by the unquenchable quest for ever-higher office; but rather that my less noble urges can be directed more appropriately to inform, amuse, entertain, occasionally inspire, and hopefully more often than not – in the words of a favorite verse of Scripture – "to do justice, seek mercy, and walk humbly with God."

It has also helped me to consider the motives of those who have tried to bring me down. I've learned that the most powerful force in public life is personal resentment. Your adversaries, in all likelihood, want something that you have, that they don't. They may feel entitled to your success, your wealth, your prestige, *your life*. Take this as an opportunity to count your blessings, to be grateful for your bounty, to understand that you are a target *because* of your enviable stature.

And for all of these reasons, go ahead and read the rest of this book. Because while you may have determined that this particular crisis doesn't deserve a response; as long as you are successful, there will always be someone looking to replace you, to tear you down – there will always be some crisis lurking around the corner.

Take it as a compliment. And be prepared for the next challenge.

STEP TWO:

Tell the Truth: Don't Even Go Near the Line

By Jeff Smith, former Missouri State Senator

"If you tell the truth; you don't have to remember anything."- Mark Twain

The first Correctional Officer (CO) I met was straight out of *Deliverance*. I came in with a young black guy who mumbled and a middle-aged Chinese man who spoke broken English, but at least I could decipher their words. The CO was harder to understand. Manchester, Kentucky is tucked in an Appalachian mountain hollow, and he had apparently never left. When he sauntered into the austere, concrete holding room and asked the Chinese man his name, the man replied, "Shoi-ming Chung."

"Sesame Chicken?" replied the CO; laughing uproariously and then repeating it twice as if it were the funniest thing he'd ever heard.

He sent me to a heavyset nurse for a battery of questions.

"Height and weight?" she asked.

"5'6", 120 pounds."

She examined my slight frame and frowned. "Education level?"

"Ph.D."

She shot me a skeptical look. "Last profession?"

"State Senator."

She rolled her eyes. "Well, I'll put it down if ya want. If ya wanna play games, play games. You'll fit right in - we got ones who think they're Jesus Christ, too."

Another guard escorted me to a bathroom without a door. He was morbidly obese and spoke gruffly in a thick Kentucky drawl. "Stree-ip," he commanded. I did. "Tern'round," he barked. I did.

"Open up yer prison wallet," he ordered.

I looked at him quizzically.

"Tern'round and open up yer butt cheeks."

I did.

"Alright, you'se good to go."

The last stop was in the office of the counselor, a wiry, compact sandy-haired man wearing a light blue polo-style shirt and a wispy mustache. He flipped through the pre-sentencing report, pausing briefly to absorb the case summary, and shook his head. "This is crazy," he said quietly, without looking at me. "You shouldn't be here. Waste of time. Money. Space."

A waste - exactly! Finally, someone agreed. But by now, it was too late.

* * *

Five years earlier, at age 29, I'd challenged the scion of Missouri's leading political dynasty; I came within 1.6% of toppling him and reaching Congress. An award-winning film chronicling the campaign titled, *Can Mr. Smith Get to Washington Anymore?* earned a cult-like following among young politicos around the country. Two years later, in 2006, I was elected to the state Senate.

Then one day in 2009, two FBI agents knocked on my door. Hours later, my political career was over, and I realized I was probably going to prison.

Let me explain how that happened – and how you can keep it from happening to you. But if you do screw up, as I did, let me then humbly offer some advice on how to recover.

* * *

It was summer 2003, and President Bush had just invaded Iraq. I was incensed about the war, distressed about the Bush tax cuts given the looming expense of boomer retirement, and passionate about education reform. Nine months after U.S. House Minority Leader Dick Gephardt declared that he would run for president instead of seeking re-election, I announced my candidacy. It was met with a deafening silence from the media, the other campaigns, and the voters.

A bevy of ambitious pols lined up to succeed Gephardt in 2004. State Representative Russ Carnahan led every poll taken. As one political science professor noted: "The Carnahan name is to Missouri what the Kennedy name is to Massachusetts." Carnahan's record was thin, his oratory lackluster and his campaign disorganized. But his family's deep ties gave him key endorsements, fundraising contacts and near-universal name ID, which was 99% in our first poll of likely primary voters. Mine was 3%; and as my press secretary Artie Harris liked to remind me, 2% of the 3% just knew *someone* named Jeff Smith – not me.

My pollster told me something he claimed he'd never told a client: He couldn't see a path to victory. Carnahan's name ID was overwhelmingly positive; people didn't distinguish him from his family. Russ's father, a popular two-term Governor who died tragically in a plane crash weeks before his election to the U.S. Senate, actually won from the grave, posthumously beating Sen. John Ashcroft. Russ's mother served in his stead. Older voters recalled his grandfather, a congressman and ambassador. Women admired his mother's service in the Senate and thrilled to his sister's candidacy for Secretary of State. This all translated into a favorable image that no negatives we tested could touch. "You might consider a different race," said my pollster. "A winnable one. How about Russ's state leg seat?" And indeed, when I sat down with a local political pundit, we talked for 45 minutes before he said, "Wait, you're running for Carnahan's seat in the state House, right?"

* * *

I started with no money and no base, ignored by elected officials, voters, journalists, and even my parents. I called every elected official in the district, beginning with every alderman and committeeperson – 45 in all. A few were wrong numbers. I left about 30 messages. One returned my call.

I didn't have much, but I had Steve Brown. Steve was my best friend and closest ally; I'd run his state House campaign in 2002, which ended in a heartbreaking 28-vote loss. We talked every day, usually more than once, about politics, sports, women. No one did more than Steve to help me. "I'm done with all of 'em, except you and Jay (Nixon, the Attorney General and future Governor)," Steve said, referring to the politicians who called him for money. "You were the only two who were there for me."

Steve's Rolodex was golden, and he rarely hesitated to use it for me. It pained me to think of his narrow loss – I wished I'd somehow done just a little more to get him over the top. But that was the past, and we focused on the present – and the future. We knew he'd run again, and when he did (which turned out to be 2008), I'd do whatever I could to help him.

With Steve's help in 2004, we ignored the many setbacks and stuck to our plan: We canvassed nightly for a year, held 93 coffees with 20-60 attendees at each, and built an army of 600 volunteers who planted 5000 yard signs at supporters' homes. But the media stuck to its narrative, too: Carnahan had a million bucks, every endorsement, a 30-point lead, and universal name ID. How could he lose?

Frustrated by this storyline, we leveraged a unique chance to circumvent it. A local filmmaker had requested access to our campaign. We granted him conditional access: In exchange for giving him the right to use all the footage after the campaign, we'd be able to use it if we asked during the campaign. So, in July, we cut a short video in an attempt to give voters substance instead of sound bites. While delivering videos, we realized that most voters we tagged as undecided were actually supporters; many requested extra videos to share with others. They'd been trying to spread the word; and without media coverage, they were just waiting for the right vehicle. They never told us they were helping; they just did it. It was the culmination of all our efforts, regular people taking ownership of the campaign.

* * *

Though we were closing quickly, we knew it wouldn't suffice unless more people had a reason to abandon the family they'd known for decades. There was information to give people pause: Carnahan's state House attendance record lagged that of 95% of his colleagues, and he'd missed critical votes. And in contrast to his boasts, he'd passed no legislation. For weeks, my press secretary Artie fed this to reporters, who ignored it. And in our frustration, in the campaign's waning days, I made a terrible mistake.

* * *

Artie and another aide burst into my call room and told me that a guy named Skip Ohlsen had approached them. Skip billed himself as a specialist in the political dark arts: opposition research and negative ads. His tentacles reached the top of the state Democratic Party; he accompanied the Lieutenant Governor to events and had stayed at the Governor's Mansion.

Skip had briefly pitched us months ago; I'd found him shady and declined. Now he was back, proposing to lead an effort highlighting Carnahan's miserable attendance record. Artie made a passionate case for approving it. "The media won't print anything negative about the Carnahans," he said. "This is the only way to show people the difference between the dad and the idiot son." We'd come a long way, but I agreed with his basic logic: We'd lose unless voters could distinguish Russ from his father.

"Whatever you guys do," I said, *"I don't wanna know the details. Understand?"*

They nodded.

I didn't know the finer points of campaign finance law, but I was pretty sure it was illegal for campaign aides to coordinate with an independent operator who planned to make an expenditure naming a candidate in the race. I was also pretty sure it happened every day, without consequences. I knew that powerful politicians (like the Carnahans) made the laws – laws that weren't designed to help upstart challengers. And I was irritated, as were the other eight candidates, that the press hadn't challenged him on issues or on his record, let alone expose him as a pale imitation of his father. Instead, they continued to highlight his establishment support, fundraising heft and huge poll lead.

I didn't know if the postcard would happen or not; we figured Skip might pocket whatever money he raised. But I barely thought about it – I had a campaign to run. One of my aides later told me that the decision weighed more heavily upon him than it did on me; he was very conflicted, though I'd been too absorbed in the campaign to recognize it. On the one hand, my aides were young men susceptible to the idea that one cut his political teeth by playing the game like the big boys. On the other, they didn't like the fact that it might require deceiving our supporters. In fact, one aide raised this concern. My aides were split, but after quickly hearing both sides, I approved it, and we all agreed to move forward – and to never speak of the matter again.

This was my first test. I wanted to win so badly that I compromised my integrity. I failed.

Yet, doubtful that Skip would actually follow through, we soon called a press conference – along with one of my opponents, pro-life state Rep. Joan Barry – to highlight Carnahan's dismal legislative attendance record. "Joan and I disagree on many things," I said. "But we agree that voters expect a leader who works as hard for this district as Congressman Gephardt has. And you can't do that if you don't show up." Joan echoed my comments. The press ignored us.

A few days later, Artie barreled into my call room. "The eagle has landed," he said archly.

"What are you talking about?" I asked. It was a week from Election Day.

Artie pulled out the postcard. It was much smaller than I'd imagined it would be, just three by five inches. Russ was pictured on a milk carton. "MISSING: RUSS CARNAHAN" it read, and in tiny print detailed his absenteeism. The design was totally amateurish – a joke, really. We laughed and shook our heads.

The next week was a blur. At 4 a.m. on Election Night, we were down about 1,000 votes, but there were still votes out. I headed home, barely able to stay awake. Suddenly my phone rang, jarring me back into consciousness. It was 7 a.m., and the final tally was in. I finished 2nd of ten, losing 22.9% to 21.3%.

Local journalist Dave Drebes summed up the race in the *Arch City Chronicle*:

"Jeff Smith didn't have a single ward endorsement. He didn't win any union endorsements...He didn't receive backing from the powerful Gephardt/Aboussie camp, or the invincible mayor...He didn't have any of the traditional forms of support. And yet Jeff Smith won the city...His campaign made endorsements look meaningless, and the Democratic machine look rusty...The Smith campaign articulated an agenda that dared to move beyond the platitudes of common political rhetoric. It resonated in this city, particularly with younger voters, new city residents, disillusioned with the politics of dumpster maintenance. They had been waiting for a breath of fresh air. This was it."

* * *

In the campaign's final days, Carnahan filed a complaint with the Federal Election Commission. The complaint argued that my campaign illegally coordinated with the postcard's producer. After the campaign, my lawyer prepared a response – an affidavit with fifteen numbered statements. Nearly all were true. One was not. "I don't know who designed, produced, printed, disseminated, or financed the postcard," it read. My lawyer handed me the affidavit.

I didn't know who actually did the first four things, but I knew Steve raised the money. I knew Artie had given Skip information about Carnahan's attendance record. That the data was publicly available didn't matter: The meeting was enough. And I knew that – like jumping into icy water – if I waited too long to sign, I wouldn't do it. I willed my hand to the paper.

This was my second test. For a variety of reasons – wanting to protect my aides from legal trouble, wanting to avoid tarnishing our acclaimed campaign, wanting to escape a huge fine when I'd just spent much of my savings on the campaign, the desire to turn the page as I prepared to move across the country – I failed badly.

* * *

After a year teaching at Dartmouth, I sought an open Missouri state Senate seat in 2006. I did not look like the district. It was 2/3 minority and overwhelmingly Protestant or Catholic. Less than 1/5 of voters had college degrees, and the median age of voters was 60. I was a 32 year-old agnostic Jew with a Ph.D.

One of my opponents sent several mailers featuring a picture of me throwing my blazer over my back, doctored to suggest a stereotypically gay limp-wristed gesture. The caption: "Jeff Smith won't be straight with us." A second opponent issued a press release calling me the "known Caucasian" in the race. An anonymous flier featuring me and a Star of David appeared. "Who will he really represent?" it asked. "North St. Louis, or Israel?"

In 2004, our desperation led me to approve Skip's postcard, and I still felt the weight of that deception. In 2006, we played it straight, responding to attacks with a midnight run – 20 of us sprinting house to house from 12-3 a.m., with fliers asking voters to ignore the negativity. We won by double digits.

The *St. Louis Post-Dispatch* reporter at my election night party summed up the vibe: "Watching Jeff's Smith's victory party, it was hard to tell whether he had won a race for the Legislature or for Student Council. College-age volunteers are drinking beer and chasing each other with water guns. A live band belted out 'Freebird.' And there was Smith playing the drums. St. Louis, meet your new senator."

Most of the city's political bigwigs who had ignored me in my first campaign showed up, all smiles and well wishes. I huddled my closest friends on the driveway and told them – almost as a warning to myself – *"You are my friends; I trust you; everyone after tonight is suspect because they may want something from me. You are friends who I can trust."*

Steve Brown was in that circle, on the driveway that night. And so it never occurred to me, years later, that he would be wearing a wire.

* * *

First, it's denial:

They're bluffing. There's no way he wore a wire. He's my best friend. Loyalty's everything to him. He couldn't do it. Not capable of it.

Then anger:

That motherfucker. After all the years we spent together, talking about politics, friendship, loyalty, trust...this? If he was gonna talk to the feds, why didn't he just cut me off instead of wearing a wire?

Then disbelief at the confluence of my bad decisions and bad luck:

Why didn't I tell Artie and Nick not to meet with Skip? Why didn't Skip just put the disclaimer on the postcard? Why didn't Russ withdraw the complaint after he won? Why did I sign that affidavit? Why did the government spend five years investigating an amateurish 3x5 postcard that didn't change the race's outcome? And...(oh shit!)...how many times in the last 2 months was he taping me and...Jesus, who knows what I said?

Once I contemplated what was about to happen to my reputation, I moved past disbelief to shame. The shame of my colleagues, my supporters, my constituents.

The shame of my parents.

They lived five minutes from my attorney's office. It was the longest five minutes of my life.

"Let's sit down," I said.

"Is everything OK?" they asked.

"Look, I made a mistake back in 2004. Remember that postcard that came out near the end of the campaign about Carnahan's attendance record? Artie and Nick had met with the guy who did it, and I OK'd it, and then lied about that on an affidavit."

"So you'll have to pay a big fine?" asked my dad.

"No, it's worse than that. I'll have to resign and maybe go to prison."

My mom's lips quivered. "I knew it from the start. Knew you'd get mixed up in something like this. I tried to tell you what politics was like..." Her voice trailed off; she stared out the window and cried.

"I'm sorry, Mom. Mom, please don't cry. It's not the end of the world. I'll be OK."

"What about us?" she asked. "Someday I hope you'll know what it's like to be a parent..."

My dad was impassive. "OK, how can we help you keep from going to prison, Jeffrey?" he asked. "How do they even know you lied? What proof could they have?"

"Steve's been wearing a wire for the last couple months."

"That sonofabitch," said my dad.

"I told you he was no good," said my mom. "But you wouldn't listen."

I breathed deeply.

"Jeffrey, do you have money for a lawyer?" Dad, always practical.

"I have some savings."

"Do you have a decent lawyer?"

"I think so. I'm going to meet him now. I'm so sorry about this." They looked much older and grayer than I'd remembered.

I hugged them and left to meet my new lawyers, Richard Greenberg and Kevin O'Malley, who greeted me with looks of grim resignation. They showed me the sentencing guidelines; I was looking at one to three years on obstruction of justice charges.

We began a dance with the Assistant U.S. Attorney, an anxious career prosecutor who would not shake my outstretched hand when we met. The dance culminated in a lengthy session with him, during which we heard the highlights of Steve's tapes. It wasn't easy listening to myself wistfully agree with Nick that we lay the blame on the now-deceased Artie, who had urged us to approve the postcard. It was harder still to imagine that these tapes could become public.

I left the courthouse with Kevin and Richard. "What'd you guys think?" I asked.

"The audio quality – it's the best I've ever heard," said Richard.

"Scale of 1-10, 10 being the worst?" I asked.

"Maybe 2.5," said Kevin, squinting. "It's some good buddies talkin', ya know? Nobody's talking about what to do with the bodies in the trunk. You're a likeable guy – it's possible you could hang a jury. But they've probably got enough for them to get you."

I agreed, and decided to plead guilty. This was my third test – knowing when the jig was up, limiting the damage, taking my medicine. I passed.

On the morning I resigned and pled, the media surrounded my house. I was numb. The courtroom was packed with media, friends, and supporters. I read an apology I'd prepared. Then I walked out onto the courthouse steps and read a statement apologizing to my family (deeply heartfelt), my constituents (heartfelt), my Senate colleagues (heartfelt), and Congressman Carnahan (at my lawyer's suggestion). I was catatonic, but I remember everyone who showed up to support me.

This was my fourth test. While I dreamed of standing at the courthouse and arguing that, despite my mistake, *it was a trumped-up charge and instead of worrying about a stupid postcard the feds oughta focus on something important like the city's sky-high murder rate!*, I did not do so. I passed.

The most salacious excerpts from the tapes flooded the airwaves. The head of the city's FBI office quivered with fury as he condemned the "textbook case of corruption," though I hadn't taken a penny in bribes. "I loved the chase," he added, describing his work. "[It] was fantastic. It was me against them. And the smarter they were...the more I enjoyed catching them." (He was soon promoted to head the FBI's Miami bureau.)

I came home to reporters and 3,000 replies to the mass email I had sent with my letter of resignation. All but eight of the replies expressed support, often tempered with disappointment; many urged me to reconsider resigning. But they didn't understand: I was now a felon, prohibited from serving.

I made a rule that day I still follow: I would never contact anyone who didn't contact me first. If someone emailed me, I would reply; if they friended me, I would accept; if they tweeted at me, I might reciprocate. I would not, however, escalate the contact level.

I made this decision not out of a desire to end friendships. In fact, I loved most of the people I met campaigning and legislating. But I didn't want to put anyone in the awkward position of having to decide whether or not to return my phone call or email. They deserved to make that decision for themselves, on their own time. Many quickly came to my side, and offered to help however they could. I asked those who offered to write letters to the judge on my behalf. Later I heard that some people were offended I hadn't reached out to ask them to write letters. They didn't realize that I didn't reach out to anyone.

A few who didn't reach out immediately wrote me in prison; since my release, people have trickled back into my life every day via LinkedIn, Facebook, Twitter, and email, with large spikes after my media appearances. I appreciate those who reconnect, even ones who, in the grand tradition of politics, resurface to ask for my help with something – I still receive an unusual assortment of constituent service requests. But I'll never forget those who came to my side immediately, in my darkest hour.

This was my fifth test. In the wake of extended public humiliation, I kept my dignity.

My attorneys asked that I be sentenced to two years of teaching history and coaching basketball at the charter school I had co-founded. It would've saved taxpayers about $175K: two years of a teacher's salary plus benefits, plus the cost of housing a federal prisoner. Several hundred people – from the state's Attorney General, Lieutenant Governor and Auditor, to my ex-girlfriend's mom, to impoverished kids I had coached – wrote impassioned letters to the judge requesting mercy. I remain deeply grateful to them.

While my co-conspirators – including my former best friend Steve – received probation according to the prosecutor's recommendation after their cooperation with him, I did not aid the prosecution's efforts to land a bigger fish, and so the prosecutor argued for a harsh sentence. The judge gave me a year and a day in prison.

* * *

I remember leaving for college with some clothes stuffed into a suitcase and a Cardinals trash can. The Raleigh-Durham airport felt sterile, impersonal. I'd never been to North Carolina and didn't know anyone at UNC. For the first time in my life, I felt alone. I was 18, and I don't recall feeling alone for another 18 years, when Teresa dropped me off in Manchester, Kentucky, on January 5th, 2010.

I'd recently met Teresa, a newly-minted Washington University MSW/MBA, and fallen in love. I was glad she drove me down; it hadn't been a given. I'd visited her at work that fateful day on the way from my parents' house to meet my lawyer; she'd moved into my house two days before that.

"Look, I have some bad news," I'd begun. "I don't have time to go into the details, but I'm gonna resign from the Senate. And I'm probably going to prison."

"What happened? Why? What's going on? Are you serious?"

"It's a long story. But right now I gotta go see a lawyer. I just wanted to tell you that I'm not coming home tonight. I wanna give you a chance to move your stuff back out without me around. Or if you want, I can help. But maybe it's easier for you if I don't? I mean, prison…you didn't sign up for this."

Her eyes had moistened as an eternity passed. "You can come home tonight," she'd said. "I'm not going anywhere." But the next month had been tough; she'd fallen into despair and returned home to Texas.

Now, outside the barbed wire fence of the intake building, I waved goodbye to her. I'd heard about guys who went in with wives, and the next thing they heard from them was a letter from a divorce attorney. Her friends thought she was crazy for staying with me. I hoped we'd make it, but I wasn't sure I'd ever see her again.

* * *

Spinning, exaggerating, parsing words and shading truths are all accepted parts of today's political dialogue. But when leaders make mistakes, they must be completely candid. Doing anything less can empower your rivals, the press, or worst of all, law enforcement, to use a false statement against you, turning a speed bump into a full-blown scandal.

There are many memorable photographs of Bill Clinton, but perhaps the most memorable is the one of a 16 year-old Clinton representing Arkansas at Boys' Nation, beaming while shaking President John Kennedy's hand. Kennedy, of course, was Clinton's role model. But there was one area in which, at a critical moment, Clinton departed from Kennedy's playbook: crisis management.

The Bay of Pigs fiasco was an unsuccessful 1961 invasion of Cuba by a CIA-trained paramilitary group who hoped to overthrow Castro's government, which routed them in three days. The media clamored for Kennedy to address the events, which he did with clarity and candor. First, he acknowledged the United States' role in the coup, and admitted the coup's failure: "The news has grown worse instead of better." Kennedy confessed surprise and disappointment in the outcome, showing a vulnerability rare among leaders, as he described "useful lessons" from the "sobering episode." He pledged to "re-examine and reorient our forces of all kinds." Last, he fully he accepted responsibility.

> *"There's an old saying that victory has a hundred fathers and defeat is an orphan...further statements, detailed discussions, are not to conceal responsibility because I'm the responsible officer of the Government."*[13]

He did not blame the CIA for insufficient planning, or his national security team for offering poor information or guidance, or anyone else for anything.

A generation later, President Clinton was confronted with his own crisis, one of somewhat less magnitude on the world stage; but which ultimately threatened his presidency and became, regrettably, a permanent blemish on his record. It involved neither the loss of life nor grand geo-political strategy, but rather, a stained blue dress. And instead of speaking candidly to the American people and admitting his mistake, he parsed words, dissembled, and gambled that stonewalling would work. It would not. Clinton would become one of just two U.S. Presidents to be impeached by the House of Representatives. And despite his otherwise excellent performance in office, he would never quite regain the trust of the legislators or aides – or the American public – to whom he swore that he "did not have sexual relations with that woman, Miss Lewinsky."

Obviously I lacked the renown of a Kennedy or Clinton. And my situation was different; it was too late for crisis management, since by the time my crisis became public, I'd already resigned. There was damage control, but most of the damage was done. My big challenge lay in post-prison re-emergence, which was a multi-stage process.

First, I let go of any lingering bitterness. One day shortly after I got to prison, a fellow inmate with whom I worked in the prison warehouse half-jokingly offered to have Steve Brown "bumped off." My inmate supervisor K.Y., a handsome, lean crack dealer from Owensboro, Kentucky, pulled me aside and told me his own story of betrayal: His brother-in-law had given up the location of K.Y.'s stash. "Damn," I sighed. "What you do to him?"

"Wasn't shit I could do, I'se already in custody," he replied. "Thought about the motherfucker for my first three years at Lexington. 'Bout killed me. But then one day I let it go. Jus like that. Cuz you can't do time like that. Your boy with the wire, you can't even *think* about the motherfucker. It'll make you crazy."

"I hear you. 'Preciate that, K.Y."

"Think about it," he said. "You gon have one fucked up year. But that motherfucker got a life sentence. He just don't know it yet." From that day on, my bitterness towards Steve dissipated.

Second, I successfully completed my sentence – three months under halfway house supervision and two years on probation. The halfway house was simultaneously easier and more complicated than I'd anticipated. Easier because – unlike prison, where staff enjoyed singling me out in an effort to marginalize me – the halfway house director smoothed the way for quick evening and weekend furloughs to my home so long as I complied with all rules. More complicated because, whereas 98% of the people with whom I was incarcerated had sold drugs, the halfway house was teeming with formerly violent criminals, some of whom boasted about already returning to their old lifestyle. Months later, I would successfully complete my probation almost a year early after my probation officer wryly told me that in the estimation of the Court, I was officially no longer a threat to society.

Third, I gradually re-engaged in Missouri policy and political circles. Affordable housing had long been an important issue to me, and I applied to consult for a statewide association consisting of groups who supported affordable housing. It was a small new group with scant funding, and they wanted help recruiting new members, raising money, and managing their government affairs. The interview was my first in a decade. Without a car post-release, I arrived in a suit, sweat-soaked from my bike ride over. "Why should we take a chance on you?" pushed a board member. "Why should we be the ones to take a hit for hiring you – wouldn't it be smarter for us to let someone else do it first?"

Maybe I was still arrogant from my Senate days. Maybe I was more candid after my lie led to trouble. Maybe I was displaying the surliness of somebody fresh out of prison. Or maybe I just had nothing left to lose. "You know, for what you're paying, you'd be getting a heckuva deal," I replied. "If you have another candidate who gets grassroots organizing, fundraising, Missouri politics, and the legislative process as well as I do, can call senators or the House Speaker to see what's going on – and isn't fresh outta prison, you should hire him." Then I thanked them for their time and left. I found out later that two of them were appalled. But they saw my logic and hired me. I'm now executive director of the Missouri Workforce Housing Association, whose membership has quadrupled and budget grown tenfold since I started.

Fourth, I applied for a professorship in the urban policy graduate program at The New School in New York City. After the initial phone interview, the search committee chair told me that he thought they'd like to bring me out to campus for an interview. I thanked him profusely for overlooking my "unique" background. "Well, frankly, we got a huge pile of applications, but yours really stuck out," he said with desert-dry wit. Thanks to the university's many open-minded people, I received the offer. In addition to accepting my past, the university has encouraged my writing as well as my affordable housing advocacy back in Missouri.

Fifth, I rediscovered writing. Jonathan Miller was the first person to reach out to me to ask if I would consider writing for his new blog, *The Recovering Politician*. Writing openly about my experience was not only therapeutic but helped lead to the publication of my work in *The Atlantic, New York Magazine, Salon, Politico,* the *Chicago Tribune*, and numerous other outlets, as well as appearances on NPR, MSNBC, and other networks.

Sixth, I began to speak to groups of public officials around the country about my experiences from an ethical perspective. How could others avoid making the same mistakes I made? Prison sucked – trust me – but the experience facilitated my ability to make others stop and consider the potential consequences of actions that may seem minor at the time.

Seventh, I began advising an array of non-profit and for-profit start-ups who were working to reform our criminal justice system to provide more education to current and just-released offenders. Having been an academic who studied the political system, a policymaker who operated in it, and a felon caught up in it, I could offer these groups a unique perspective – and perhaps, in some karmic way, repay the guys who'd befriended and protected me in Kentucky.

Finally and most importantly, I married Teresa, and we had a beautiful baby boy – with a second on the way. We live with two mischievous mutts she rescued, and whom I frequently re-rescue after they nip at our son Charlie, and Teresa threatens to return them. I've learned that nothing gives you perspective like the sweetness of your baby's breath at dawn.

The final stage of crisis management is often reparative – how do you repair your relationships with people you care about, how do you repair your public image, and perhaps prerequisite to the above, how do you repair yourself in a way that allows you to move on from crisis and humiliation to reinvent yourself in a way that stays true to the best of who you are?

I always find great irony – and sometimes a bit of tragedy – in the stories of disgraced pols who rush for immediate reinvention in the same ego-nurturing and soul-crushing arena that got them in trouble in the first place. It is as if the Mark Sanfords and Anthony Weiners of the world have determined that the artificial politico personas they have so painstakingly created are indeed the only versions of themselves that they can still recognize. It seems they don't understand that true redemption requires you to hit the pause button, to sublimate ambition and reflect on what truly matters.

Don't get me wrong, prison was awful. But it forced me to pause and reflect, and thus gave me an advantage over the Sanfords and Weiners on the road to recovery. It helped me realize that the only way to ever shed my baggage would be to embrace the lessons my crisis taught me in my future roles as a teacher, a scholar, an advocate, a friend, and a husband.

The prison where I spent most of 2010 didn't have an actual fence but was mostly enclosed by natural barriers – we sat in the bowl of a canyon with a steep cliff on the sides. At the prison edge was a boundary line. During orientation, you are told not to cross it. The CO leading orientation may warn you about the snipers in the guard towers, just waiting for a stray inmate to make a run for it. And you awaken each morning to the sounds of COs taking target practice at the adjacent shooting range.

One thing is certain: If you end up going near the line, and a sniper imagines you to have crossed it, or gets a little trigger-happy, or is just having a bad day, it could be all over for you. And when they report your death (trust me again here), no forensic investigator will conclude that you were actually – narrowly – on the right side of the line. You'll just go down as another escapee intercepted by a lawman's bullet. So you learn quickly not to go *anywhere near* the line.

In the haze of a campaign, when you are sleep-deprived, frayed, and under intense pressure from donors, staff, volunteers, voters, and yourself, it can be easy to lose sight of the larger picture. And in business, near the closing of a huge sale, merger, or acquisition; or in sports, in the heat of battle; or in your personal life, it can be tempting to seek an extra edge, shade a truth, cut a corner. Making that mistake cost me my political career, my reputation (temporarily, I hope), and a precious year of my life.

That's why – long before that climactic moment of decision – it is best to not go anywhere the line, for leaders who are surrounded by people closely familiar with their boss' ethical probity are unlikely to be presented with the chance to make a fatefully poor decision.

* * *

The other day I carried my bike up out of Penn Station on the way downtown to substitute teach for a colleague. Starting down 7th Avenue, I felt ice pellets whipping against my face, thanks to an Arctic mix of near-freezing temperature and gale-force winds. I became annoyed. *Why did I ride my fucking bike today? If I was gonna ride, why didn't I just lock it up at Penn Station? Why did I even agree to sub for some guy I barely know?*

And then suddenly it hit me, hit me harder than sleet or wind, harder than a double-decker tourist bus:

I was free.

Wind? Ice pellets? Who gave a fuck?!

I was on my way to teach brilliant grad students, in the world's most vibrant city; and when I finished, I would be free to go home and snuggle up with my wife and kid. I flashed back to my year of backbreaking work in the prison warehouse, and the prison beefs I got in, and the human misery I saw, and the looks on the faces of Teresa and my parents and brother when they visited. What I wouldn't have given on any of those days to ride out of that prison into a frigid sleet thrashing my face, free to ride anywhere I liked!

At that instant on 7th Avenue, I knew that I would never again take any of it for granted. **This, I realized, was my final test: coming out on the other side, understanding how my experience made me stronger; knowing what is truly important in life; and emerging as a better teacher, advocate, friend, father, and husband than I'd have otherwise been.**

I agreed to write this chapter in hopes that you learn these lessons without losing a year of your life to prison and years more rebuilding your career – and without putting your loved ones through the strain I put mine through.

STEP THREE:

Lean Into, and Learn from, Your Crisis

By John Y. Brown, III, former Kentucky Secretary of State

My own dark night of the soul. Without a crisis manager to guide me.

At the age of 22, most of my friends had graduated college and were beginning to wear suits and ties and dress shoes and carry a sleek umbrella when it rained, as they went to work at enviable places like accounting and law firms and growing businesses and established organizations.

I was doing none of those things and felt ostracized and dismissed by my peers and friends and loved ones who had run out of patience with me. I was out of all of my "second chances."

Hope from others had been displaced with sadness, concern and eventually disgust. Friends were calling my parents telling them I needed help and that they were worried for my safety. One of my old friends had just visited me while he was back in town and saw me in shambles, in a deliberately dark and dank apartment wearing only my dingy robe (ironically decorated with Roman Empire images), as I sat disheveled, unshaven and un-bathed amid a sea of empty vodka, bourbon and beer bottles.

I had squandered my last few jobs and dropped out of college for three consecutive semesters from three different colleges. When my friend asked me what I was going to do next, I joked in my own macabre way that "I was torn between starting my own business and committing suicide." I laughed through my pain, but he had only a look of concern and sad confusion.

A few days after that, my father came to my apartment late on a rainy Sunday afternoon and knocked furiously on my door. He knew something was very wrong, but I kept the shades drawn, lights out and refused to answer.

Finally, the knocks became kicks at the base of the door. Followed by more knocks that eventually trailed off with a sense of defeat I had come to recognize from others trying to help me. It was my father, a man whose time was precious and I'd always wanted more of; and I finally opened the door and walked outside. The bottom of the door had scuffmarks from his shoes; and my father was in his car, and I got in the passenger side.

I said, "I've screwed up, Dad. I've really screwed up, and my life is a mess." My voice cracked, and I looked down dejectedly as I began crying tears of desperation. My father was a man of action who had built Kentucky Fried Chicken, owned the Boston Celtics, and just finished serving a term as Kentucky's Governor. He wasn't accustomed to not having a quick answer to solve any problem that faced him. But he was bewildered, too. I remember him saying "we'll get through it," and that he would help find a way. He had heard of treatment centers for problems like mine, and maybe that's what I needed to do. He said, "You are my flesh and blood, and the blood that runs through your veins runs through mine, too. We'll figure this out. I love you and want to help however I can."

But, again, there were no quick fixes for how to deal with

my problem.

A few weeks after that, I moved back home with my mother, since I was not functional at either work or school and unable to care for myself with the kind of minimal self-care expected of some my age. I was a listless, beleaguered and bewildered soul. Mostly, ironically, confused. I had no idea what was really wrong with me or what next to do. I just knew something was terribly wrong, and I was out of solutions and out of any help from friends or family.

One of the last nights I was in my apartment (an apartment, by the way, that the exterminator who visited routinely once told me was the worst kept apartment of the 4,400 he serviced monthly), I was standing alone in my bedroom trying to come up with a new plan. I looked at the world map hanging above my bed and decided what I needed to do was move.

Again.

But this time, not to another city or state, but to an entirely new country. I figured moving to England made the most sense because I didn't know how to speak any foreign languages; and I had heard they served beer at room temperature there, which would mean I wouldn't drink as much of it as I did the cold beer in the US. And it further seemed that living in what was called a "flat" instead of an "apartment" sounded more manageable to me.

My only other plan really wasn't a plan at all, but what I had come to view as a possible way out. I recalled watching a news special several months earlier about Robert F. Kennedy's son David dying of a drug overdose. His family and friends said it was a "tragedy," and that David was a talented and good-hearted young man who was misunderstood and gotten into trouble with drugs.[14] David, I imagined, had been in a dark and desperate place and felt there was no way out, much like I was feeling. But in dying, he seemed to have found a way to make his life legacy "tragic," and an example of "unrealized potential," rather than a devastating disappointment.

That legacy actually occurred to me as an option I should remember. I don't think I ever was capable of suicide, but Nietzsche wrote that the option of suicide had gotten many a person through a dark night.[15] I did, at least, understand what he meant by that.

At the most basic level, I decided that my continuing series of bad luck endured in recent years was the cause of me drinking excessively. And that if I could just get a single small break, things would begin to turn around for me. But every turn in my life was not into a brighter corner, but into a darker and more desperate corner.

Turns out, I had it backwards. I had the consistent series of misfortunes because I was drinking excessively. And now, I couldn't stop, and needed to drink daily just to survive the overwhelming disappointment my life had become.

I wasn't living, but merely enduring day to day.

* * *

When I was first asked to write a chapter for a crisis management book for my good friend, Jonathan Miller, I thought: "What an extraordinary opportunity to create a thoughtful, useful and ethical commentary that identifies some of the most valuable coping mechanisms for businesses, political leaders, celebrities, and – most important of all – just regular folk like the rest of us, to manage successfully when our lives are beset by a personal or professional crises."

Each chapter would be written by a different author and identify a specific kind of coping strategy personally experienced by the author. These strategies would, ideally, lay out an approach not only to "survive" a crisis – but also to navigate the crisis and learn from it; and, eventually, even come out the better because of it.

The idea, in part, is a paradigm shift in our thinking about crisis. Instead of the most common responses to crisis (i.e., denial, blaming, minimizing or simply ignoring – think the ostrich, with its head in the sand), the hope is that after reading this book, the reader will be encouraged not to turn away from crisis, but turn toward it. To grab the crisis situation, as it exists, pull it up by the collar, hold it up to your face, and stare it down courageously, candidly and, yes, savvily – based not on theories, but recommendations that have worked for the authors and come from the crucible of actual life experience.

I remember hearing as a college student in the late 80s a story about American resilience that has stayed with me. At the time, America was feeling threatened by Japan's explosive economic growth and seeming technological superiority.

A fellow student posited a theory he had recently read about suggesting that America would remain economically superior to Japan – not because of our brain power or creativity or hard work or even innovation – but rather because, as a culture, we are better at "bouncing back" from failure. We are, as part of our culture, more resilient and better at accepting failure as an inevitable part of success; and when crisis (small, medium or catastrophic) occurs, the crisis is viewed merely as an obstacle, a speed bump, a part of the obstacle course we are on that we have to navigate as we work to find a better way. To build a better mousetrap, as the saying goes.

Whether or not this theory is actually true, I grabbed hold of the story and adopted it as part of my belief system. And I believe it is sound reasoning and a good life philosophy to, well, embrace adversity and make it our teacher, rather than our master. I believe that the person who can expect and emerge stronger from setbacks is always more likely to ultimately prevail.

I like visual images to reinforce beliefs I hold. To go back to Aesop's fable about the tortoise and the hare, we learned that "slow and steady wins the race." That is sage advice; but an even better and more applicable life lesson that I have observed in my life over and over again is that "moderately and consistently fast, coupled with the ability to overcome setbacks" wins the race more often still.

So think of a resilient turtle with a high emotional IQ who not only plodded along consistently, but also overcame a series of predictable setbacks as he crosses the finish line ahead of the hyper-kinetic and gifted hare, which hadn't yet learned to navigate the terrain.

So, what exactly is a setback and how does one bounce back from it? They come in different shapes and sizes and require a specific type of response tailored to each type of crisis.

One of my favorite bosses, advises me regularly, "To either win – or fail spectacularly trying." We always laugh when he says that: laughing knowingly at the wisdom of trying our hardest, laughing nervously at the prospect of failing spectacularly. The key, I believe, is learning to develop an appreciation for the inevitability of some form of failure(s).

Not so much developing an "appetite for failure." That both sounds like and is bad planning. But to develop a strategic vision that includes missteps, miscalculations and, yes, even spectacular failures as possibilities in any worthwhile endeavor; and when these setbacks occur, deal with them as part of the "overall strategic process."

That requires courage and wisdom that displaces the more immature and cowardly view that setbacks can't be allowed to happen; or, that if they happen, can't be acknowledged without acknowledgement being viewed as a concession of failure.

An especially difficult or high step we have to take, as our walk up a real life set of unpredictable stairs, doesn't mean we have failed. It just means it's starting to get interesting; and we now have to turn off our autopilot and dig a little deeper, and tap into that part in us that lives for a challenge.

Think of it this way: A short story by Flanery O'Connor has a scene in which several boys are on a journey and encounter a high wall they believe they can't ascend. One boy takes off his hat and throws it over the wall and says to the other boys, "Now I have no choice. I have to find a way over."[16] I love that sentiment.

But is that Puritan impulse to work harder and overcome obstacles the right mindset for combating every life crisis? In other words, is this chapter going to be a predictable cheer lead, talking through how not to let adversity get you down and how to use tried and true techniques to overcome setbacks?

It was going to be. But once I started writing, I kept getting pulled into a different direction.

So, no, it's not going to me that kind of chapter. In fact, it's going to be about viewing some rare and seemingly catastrophic setbacks in a very counter-intuitive way that I believe is worth considering as a response in certain extreme circumstances. And maybe, as it was for me, not only the prudent response, but also a personally defining response, that not only helped me emerge from the crisis but also redefined who I am and my life mission.

To be clear, we are not talking here about the run of the mill setback – but rather, as my boss liked to call them, the spectacular setback. The kind of setback that can't be hidden or ignored. That is a glorious failure that others (our competitors and detractors) are not only whispering about, but also discussing out loud (even though we struggle to admit that). The kind of failure that is so big that almost everyone around us has noticed and acknowledged it – and eventually, and finally, we have to admit and deal with it ourselves.

It's sometimes when our best laid plans suddenly and unexpectedly implode. Or maybe we've been blind to the fact that for far too long we've been hoping against hope that something would work out that obviously isn't going to. Or maybe we just "blew it" – through our own arrogance or vanity or irresponsibility, we failed ourselves.

What do we do when these sorts of crisis occur?

There's a great scene from John Steinbeck's novel *Cannery Row* in which the protagonist, Doc, a marine biologist, is talking to a friend and vagrant and describes his frustration with failing to succeed in his life's work experiment for 27 years, and worries about his status as a biologist among his peers. The vagrant, Mack, replies, "Doc, why don't you just give up?"[17]

It's wise advice if it is bullheadedness and pride causing a failure, as you attempt to achieve something far past the time it can realistically occur, and now has become a situation of throwing good money (and time) after bad. Your main task here is shrinking your pride and expanding your humility until both intersect with reality.

But the final kind of failure is a different sort – it's the spectacular, in your face, over the top, unforgettable, humiliating and soul-gnawing failure that leaves you, once you are awake, to the reality, in a pile of your own ashes. It's the kind when you swing for the fences, you not only strike out; but before the third strike, foul the ball and run headlong toward third base instead of first, as the crowd roars with laughter, and you end up on the front page of the sports section the next day. The kind of failure that calls not for redirection but profound reassessment: reassessment not of the situation, but of who you are and what your purpose is in life.

The kind of failure experienced by a friend of mine who worked long and hard hours toiling away in college majoring in biology so he could one day be a doctor – and fainting the first week of medical school at his first sighting of blood. His fellow students ridiculed him, and he decided that after all his plans and hard work medical school wasn't for him and dropped out.

Was he a failure? It sure sounds like it. Until I tell you the rest of the story.

The following year he enrolled in law school and went on to graduate first in his law school class, becoming one of the most respected attorneys in his field where he practices in Lexington, Kentucky. But he didn't force his way through medical school, which he wasn't suited for. He redirected his life in a different direction as a result of the crisis and found a new and better path.

The crisis, you could say, introduced this man to himself. He embraced the man he met and built a life consistent with what he learned about himself. Crisis has a way of working like that.

And then there's a variation of this sort of free fall disappointment and devastation that doesn't have a tidy happy ending like simply changing careers – but veers off in a totally unexpected direction. A direction the person in question never planned on taking or would ever believe he or she would take under the most unlikely of circumstances. It's the sort of failure that one can rise above and move on from the heap of ashes surrounding them, but cannot approach this particular type of adversity with any of the traditional or conventional methods. Navigating these dark and seemingly catastrophic moments of truth is not so much a matter of the head, but of the heart.

To get to a place you've never been, you have to go a way you've never gone. It is a bewildering journey based on faith and instinct, not clever maneuverings. And, in the end, it's not a destination that you find, but rather it finds you. And in that sense it is, in my opinion, how we deal with these sorts of failures can potentially be the most profound and transformative life experiences we are capable of having.

I don't mean to overwhelm you with metaphors, but they are the only way of truly describing the fall and re-emergence from such devastating life setbacks. The road out is a sort of blind journey or leap of faith. The path is only lit a few feet ahead as you walk, but you keep trudging along faithfully and alone (because no one can really go there with you, not even a crisis manager). It is a journey inside that, if successful, ties you back to something deep inside you that you either lost or never found but is essential.

And that if you keep walking step by solitary step, you may discover the road back. For your redemption is also the road to your own salvation.

* * *

A few months after moving home with my mother, I was up late alone the night of October 18th, 1985, watching the movie *Reuben, Reuben*...again. A movie about a rumpled, drunken curly-haired poet who had traded whatever talent he once had to sponge off others whom he was happy to take advantage of – and time was running out for him.

I suspect at the time that I was still deluded enough to believe I was watching the movie because I related to something noble in his character: some potential he had but was throwing away. In retrospect, however, I really related to the excessive drinking and manipulation of others; and mostly, frittering away a life that could be much more. In the final scene, Reuben attempts suicide, and before he can change his mind, accidentally dies.

That night, at around 2:30am, after the movie ended, I walked a handful of empty bottles of booze out to the condo's garbage chute and ceremoniously dropped them down one by one. I said incredulously maudlin and sincere sad farewells to each bottle. "We had a great run, pal!" I whispered to the empty bottle of Chivas Regal, and then again to the empty fifth of Stolichnaya Vodka. And so on.

I listened as each empty bottle dropped 16 floors to its

final death, splattering into shards in the dumpster below. I suppose, although I wasn't aware of it at the time, I felt my life was splattering into tiny pieces, broken beyond recognition, as I turned and walked back inside.

I didn't know what would happen. I just knew I was done and was, finally, willing to reach out for help from that dark and lonely place that felt like black hole I had fallen into and become numb to ever finding a way out from.

The next day I called for help. I asked for help, not out of "good strategic planning," nor a desire for "self-improvement," nor on the advice of a "life coach," but mostly because my mother had told me I could no longer live with her if I didn't. And I was horrified at the idea of having no place to go and no one to turn to. It was one of the bravest things my mother has ever had to do.

And it helped save my life.

I have not had a drink of alcohol since. That was over 27 years ago.

Before picking up the phone the next day, every fiber in my being cried out against doing so. I had plans for myself. Big plans. And to admit this sort of humiliating defeat at such a young age would ruin my life and all my grand plans along with it.

"An alcoholic!?!" I thought to myself. "My life is over. Done. My dreams all shattered. Who wants an alcoholic for anything?" But I picked up the phone and called anyway. Because I had no other options left. It was, I was certain, the most awful day of my life.

What I was convinced was the lowest, most pathetic and reprehensible moment of my life was, in fact, something very different. What I was convinced was the "worst thing that could ever happen to me" (becoming an alcoholic) was, in retrospect, after placing it in God's hands, the very best thing that could have happened to me.

Not only did the call for help signify the end of my drinking, but the beginning of a new life. The less I tried to run from it; the more I was blessed by it. At first I only could muster the fortitude to admit my crisis. Then, after some time had passed, I was able to accept it. And by continuing a little longer along this different path, I came to approve of the wound that caused me to humble myself and reach out for help.

I learned that we are not at our weakest when asking for help. But at our most human. It is the moment when we open our soul for true and lasting change…and connect with another in the most remarkable way two people can interact: One beggar telling another beggar where to find the bread.

After that, my life stabilized and I build an entirely new one. I took a minimum wage job tutoring kids in middle and high school and went back to college myself. Over the next three years, I had a 3.9 GPA and got accepted to law school, where I also graduated with honors. I married the love of my life, and we started a magnificent family.

I had success in the business world and decided to run for statewide political office in 1995, running to be Kentucky's Secretary of State. Rumors began surfacing about my past drinking; and about two months before the general election, I was asked point blank if I was an alcoholic.

I didn't dodge the question, but addressed it appropriately and honestly. I released a response that said I was indeed an alcoholic; and that 10 years earlier, I had sought help and had not had a drink of alcohol since.

I further added that I wasn't ashamed of this fact, but considered it the most significant aspect of my life – and wore my sobriety as a badge of honor, not a mark of shame.

I didn't say that in a boastful way at all, but in a truthful way that meant I had made peace with this fact about myself, and it had made me a better person. I figured that if I weren't at peace with this part of my past, I couldn't ask Kentucky's voters to be. But I was at peace; and that's what my message communicated. I concluded that there was nothing more that needed to be said, and I was moving on to discussing only policy issues related to the campaign.

I worried how this disclosure would impact the campaign. The story broke and was picked up by the Associated Press and ran in every major Kentucky newspaper. An editorial ran in the state's largest newspaper that said they admired people who faced problems head on, and that I was a person who was viewed by those who knew me best as honest, hardworking and full of potential.

I didn't have to deny my demons or unpleasant past. I had gotten to a point where I could reach out and shake hands with that part of myself and even embrace it. No longer fighting, but incorporating into myself as I am today.

* * *

I was reminded years later of former Iowa Governor, Harold Hughes. In the final debate of his 1962 gubernatorial campaign, his opponent, late in the debate, waived a document at the camera and said sternly, glowering at Hughes: "Here is a copy of an arrest for public intoxication, Mr. Hughes. How do you explain yourself and how can a person with your past be fit to serve the people of Iowa as their next governor?" Or words to that effect.

Hughes' response was from the heart, and not a defensive answer replete with excuses, blaming or minimizing of the event in question. Hughes responded with an answer that said (I am paraphrasing), "That is correct. I was cited for public intoxication a decade ago. But you missed several other arrests in Alabama, Florida, and Georgia about that time. I am what's known as an alcoholic. That all happened over 10 years ago, and I have not had a drink since then; and with God's help, I hope that alcohol never passes my lips again. Now, I'd like to get back to the debate and discuss the policy issues affecting the people of Iowa."[18] Hughes won by a landslide.

* * *

Whatever our dark moments and desperate experiences lead us into is not as important as where they can lead out to. They may leave us with a slight limp, but we learn to adapt and thrive, limp and all. And thrive because we are better, deeper, wiser, and most of all, experienced and authentic. Whatever we strive to be in life, nothing is more powerful than being our authentic glorious little selves as we were intended to be. And pick up our tools and do our work in our small corner of the world in the role we were meant for. And as part of my wound and rehabilitation, I have had the chance – no, the honor – of occasionally helping others who are in the clutch of a crises with alcohol like I was 27 years ago.

Which leads to what may be the most valuable lesson I can share with the reader about emerging from crisis. The ultimate lesson I learned, and try daily to remember, is that I stand the tallest not when I reach to see how high I can grab something for myself for others to see; but rather how low I am willing to stoop to help a fellow human being in some small way. When no one is watching.

* * *

I will close this chapter with a wonderful fable retold by poet Robert Blye in his book *Iron John*, in which he explains symbolically the phenomenon I just tried describing:[19]

In the tale, a boy approaches a caged wild man in the courtyard of his family home. He wounds his finger opening the cage. The wild man then lifts the boy to his shoulders and carries him back to his forest and leaves the boy beside a sacred golden pond and tells him not to put anything into the pond. The boy instinctively dips his wounded finger in the pond and it is instantly healed and turns golden – not as a curse, but as a sacred reward. The wounded finger symbolizes wounds we all have.

Later, the boy leans over the stream to look into his eyes and sees another being that is his positive shadow. This twin, or better side that he sees, represents the boy's unknown and rich potential to grow into the full and sacred person he wants to be.

As he gazes at his potential self, his hair falls forward into the stream and turns golden, too. The wound becomes his secret gold that was the beginning and basis for a renewed life and better self. And it all started with a wound that resulted from a bold endeavor of opening the cage.

I hope when overwhelming crisis beset us, that we don't hunker down and close up, but rather open up and reach out. And begin the long journey of reconstruction and renewal. I hope we find our wounds and embrace them.

And eventually, when the time comes, dip the wounded part of ourselves into the golden river and discover how the darkest moments in our life can be transformed to become the brightest beacon for others that we may one day help – as they open up and reach out from their dark place.

And finally, and most importantly, I hope we do this not because it is good business or good strategy. But simply because it is good to do good to another human being in need. Period. And we'll have our crisis to thank for teaching us that.

STEP FOUR:

Make an Emotional Connection

By Jason Atkinson, former Oregon
State Senator

I held the phone close standing on my front porch, in my favorite old jeans and faded Black Crowes concert t-shirt.

The anti-inflammatories were running unusually late. The reporter on the other line was a good one, old-fashioned "just give me the facts man" kinda guy, which is why I called him first. Sure, I could trust him to get the story right, but I've learned to protect my loose words from giving him reason to take me down a tangent. This time, I needed his credibility to set the tone of the other stories that I knew would follow. I wouldn't say we were friends; I'd say we were two professionals who knew the rules of engagement and appreciated each other's skills.

Second-guessing every thought inside a pregnant pause, my brain knew I was doing the right thing. The political animal that whispers my name, regardless of my attempts to kill him, was yelling the opposite.

What I had to say would reverberate across the state. I wasn't simply struggling to survive a severe physical wound;

political competitors in my own party would be rushing to declare my political future dead. The other party would spin out backhanded complements, and say something to the effect "we respect Atkinson's decision and think it will now be even harder to beat us," or something more flowery.

Standing outside was an accomplishment in itself, yet it offered no reward. I was human, with real life stopping my ambition to serve; and I knew the fencing match the reporter and I were starting did not represent who and what I was really going through.

But I needed to connect with people. I needed to find a shared value, good or bad.

I needed to make **an emotional connection**.

* * *

I love the rider and the elephant analogy: The rider is the rational mind that thinks he is directing the elephant. The elephant is the emotional mind that allows the rational mind to lead, unless a mouse – or life, or crisis – scares the elephant, who then goes wherever he wants.[20]

The rational rider thinks he's in charge. The emotional elephant has all the power and actually makes the moves, but is afraid to lead unless it's a crisis.

Politicians and their PR teams respond to crisis the exact same way as corporate leaders and their PR teams: We talk in the rational. We talk in absolutes that make logical sense. We employ "power" words, play one-upmanship, and protect the manicured brand. The rules of engagement state that the goal is to make my rational more credible than the other side's rational.

Sadly, both sides lose credibility and any hope of connecting with the audience.

There is a homey comfort inside the rational. After all,

powerful people like to steer the elephant, right?

When a crisis hits, the rational whip out the facts, the studies, the experts, talk-to-the-hand-the-hand-is-listening, and...wait a minute...what if the crisis is a highly publicized scandal, an intimate family dispute, or a decision you made that hurts people? What if it's a medical crisis?

Do you really want to rely on your ability to be the rider when your insides are torn up? Your emotions are running scared? Your heart is broken? You're the one who is guilty? You have to confess you've told a lie, and now you're really telling the truth?

Still want to ride?

* * *

There are only three causes of crisis: money, health or poor decisions.

That's it.

It always boils down to those three; and whether you're a CEO, or someone working two jobs on their second marriage, with young kids, soccer practice, and aging parents – it is always those three.

And a critical step in surviving each of these kinds of crises is to make an emotional connection with your target audience.

So here are three ways to make an emotional connection with real people when it's crisis management time:

1. Be Honest

In a time of crisis, the emotional elephant looks for shared values – values every human being has or has experiences with.

The root-shared value is honesty. The elephant goes

there first. Plausibility, believability, likelihood, authority, integrity -- all of these words follow honesty. Complete honesty.

Complete honesty goes against our grain as people. We are genetically, physiologically, and spiritually nervous about the completeness of honesty. Remember why the Garden of Eden went from a nudist colony to fig leaf modesty? God asked, "Where are you two?" and Adam and Eve came back with a guilty look and wearing produce.

Complete honesty. Without it, making the emotional connection becomes thrice as hard.

Lance Armstrong confessed on Oprah he had doped to win seven tours, but didn't dope for his last three years of his cycling career.

Was he completely honest? Nope.

Armstrong doped the whole time and was couching his answers on his last three years to protect himself legally. The truth is that he was a litigious bully who walked on the moral high ground of the Livestrong charity. Unfortunately, he was not honest for years, and his credibility eroded to the point that many thought he was being forced to confess. In the end, he made matters far worse.

Armstrong failed to connect because he was rational. He appeared defiant, arrogant, and above it all. Never in the interview did he admit bullying, hurting people personally and professionally. Never did he say, "I'm sorry I let so many people down." Not once did he ask for forgiveness. He reached for the fig leaf.

Bill Clinton didn't want to come clean either. He lied, fought, was impeached, and then finally, like Lance, was forced to own up to the scandal.

What was different?

Clinton ultimately was completely honest, and he demonstrated it by naming names. His apology was to his own family, the Lewinsky family, and the American people. Critics aside, he told people he made a mistake, tried to cover it up, got caught and was really sorry.

He connected because the fact is that everyone, every human, has followed that path at one time in his or her life. Stealing candy from the store in second grade, all the way to the affair, Clinton was real, like everyone…completely.

Don't believe me? Take it from former Armstrong teammate, Tyler Hamilton:

> *"I can speak from experience that telling the truth feels so good. It's totally changed my life. I didn't have much to look forward to before I told the truth. I still wish I'd made the right choice but I'm really excited about moving forward with the second part of my life. I couldn't have said that two years ago. It's the same with Lance. His future is going to be so much greater if he tells the truth."[21]*

Being honest, of course, doesn't mean you have to tell everything. Unless you've chosen Jerry Springer to present the crisis to the public, it's OK not to air all the family's dirty laundry. Airing everything at once appears like you're not being honest and trying to deflect. Bill Clinton spared us from the details.

Understand that the public respects privacy, as long as it's transparent:

- A child in the hospital; people understand.

- We will make this right, but we need to know what happened first; people understand.

- Time to restore one's family; people understand.

- This is an on-going legal case; people don't understand.

- I've told you everything; people don't understand.

- It's just a small procedure; people don't understand.

And don't ever become a no commenter. "No comment" is the worst comment. No comment allows the crisis to define itself. No comment tells the audience there is a lot more to the story. No comment is like yelling, "I'm not going to tell you the whole truth." Take it from former Congressman Charlie Wilson, a famous "no commenter":

> "It's embarrassing to say but it took a subpoena by the federal investigators to knock me over the head and get me to tell the truth. It was the best thing that ever happened. I really didn't realize it. I knew going in that I was going to tell to the truth but I didn't realize that telling the truth would be so good for me."[22]

2. Establish Credibility, Quickly

Credibility levels everything. Credibility makes you touchable, real, and human. Credibility allows you to talk directly to real people who hold all the cards. If you own your position, you'll establish credibility. Act like the CEO, the vice president, the Senator, which is what people think you are.

A few more tips to be credible in a crisis, when it's your public crisis:

- Be relatable. Two words that say it all.

- Don't dress like your audience. (Unless its part of your public reputation already).

- Don't use slang.

- Unless you're Anna Wintour or Bono, don't wear sunglasses.

- Don't use words you don't already use.

- Take a big breath and talk slow.

- Talk slow- it so important, it's in here twice.

- Be yourself.

Most importantly, you have to be credible quickly. Why is speed so important? Several reasons, but the obvious is the nature of media. If you don't establish quick credibility, someone else affected by the crisis will. We live in the instant in 2013, not the 24-hour news cycle of 2003.

Another reason for speed is more personal. A major crisis has a huge effect on the mental abilities of people in the crisis. Establishing credibility early in the crisis builds the confidence of the people involved.

3. **Be the Audience**

What is most credible is finding the shared values of being human. Empathy, honesty, pain, pride, suffering, victory, loss, worry – these are common connections. In a crisis, find the way to connect to people on the human level ASAP.

That sounds dumb, you think? That might be because you think the audience is dumb. Let me ask a few questions:

- Are you a parent?

- Are you upside down on your house?

- Has cancer touched your family?

- Have you ever had to say sorry?

- You don't like being fooled either?

- Do you have an aging parent?

- You don't like people who pass the buck?

- Think men should be gentlemen?

- Believe there is a glass ceiling that needs to be smashed?

- You are in charge, aren't you?

- You are ultimately responsible even though you had no idea, right?

In fact, the audience is *smart.* 99.9% of people in politics and high-level business get into a crisis and think the audience is dumb, gullible, and lazy – and that is a disaster. People know bull from steak. They listen to words, watch body language and make snap decisions if the person is honest and credible. That decision is based on whether *they found a shared value in how you handled the crisis.*

The audience might not understand the legal nuances, but they know their home equity evaporated. They might not be up to speed with how the weather in Utah turns off the lights in Iowa, but they do understand their lights are off. They don't care about the tides, but do want the oil out of the water. They make instant decisions knowing the difference in the "I'm sorry" face, "I'll clean it up" face, and "I don't want to tell you, now where'd I put those fig leafs?" face.

Sometimes you have to get down to the level of real people while maintaining the respect of your public position and connection on a shared value. President Bush on top of the rubble of the World Trade Center. President Bush not getting out of the helicopter during Katrina. At which forum did he make the emotional connection? At which forum did he find the shared value "suffering"?

That's why it is so important to connect on some relatable level. You have something in common with your audience, but it can't be your wrecked car and their toothache. You may never say it, but the emotion you choose to connect on has to be level with whom you're talking to. There is only one Tiger Woods, but he could have connected as a kid with a dream to be the best. He could have said he was changing his focus on life and wanted to use his wealth for the good. Real people have dreams. Real people want to be the good guy. A big shot of humility buttressed with honesty, goes a long way, trust me!

Think like your audience. Do they think the politician sitting in a classroom reading to kindergarteners, hugging the rental golden retriever, or wearing a cowboy hat when they drive a Lexus is credible? No, that's bull.

Real people see right through plastic veneer; they feel disconnected from the logical rider talking points. People who are in public positions are largely seen as un-relatable, and being a phony trying to be relatable hurts you worse.

Be relatable by finding the shared value.

* * *

The Kurds of Northern Iraq had been abandoned by the western world for over a century: Their homeland was carved up after both world wars, the Baath Party rise, the horrific Anfal Genocide, and Saddam Hussein's backlash after the first Gulf War.

The first President Bush established a no-fly zone to prevent Saddam from trying to destroy every living Kurd, which gave them a platform for freedom. The Kurdistan Regional

73

Government (KRG) was established with a Prime Minister, a President, a Parliament, its own security force, and most importantly – for the first time since Noah – the right to vote…for everyone.

After the second Iraqi war, the Kurds felt they were going to be abandoned again if the US removed troops, leaving them venerable to Baath Party attacks from Baghdad, which as far as the Kurds were concerned was a different country.

The Kurds had a major crisis.

They wanted to scream out with rider logic of why they are the best foundation for democracy in the Middle East. If Americans knew the history, knew the real story, surely the crisis could be averted!

I worked with the team that advised Kurdistan. My associates thought like the elephant. Our team knew that rider logic would get buried in the political noise of Washington, and that it would never get the attention of the White House, which was the decision-maker.

So we went back. Back to finding the shared value to establish credibility.

The team rebranded Kurdistan: "The Other Iraq." We created a TV spot that ran in the United States and in Great Britain with a simple message: "Thank You, America."

That's it. No ask, no appeal, no "don't abandon us again."

Those media days were driven by images of Iraqis in Baghdad fighting US troops with roadside bombs and other tactics of terror to get the US to leave. But in northern Iraq it was different. We knew that we would connect with Americans on the common value of gratitude.

The results surprised us all: The new brand was repeated by reporters, including on *60 Minutes*. In the end, a Pro-Kurd movement was organized with members of Congress; and today there is a US presence to ensure the KRG government takes hold.

"Thank you, America" was honest, credible, and we knew the audience.

* * *

I stared working in Iraq after I lost an election to become Governor of Oregon. I postponed one trip when my wife was diagnosed with cancer. After she beat the disease, I returned to Iraq.

A few months later, in my shop, I was nearly killed by a .38 handgun I've still never seen. It cut my femoral artery and I lay bleeding...I was told, 90 seconds from death. Discussions of amputations and custom wheelchairs when I woke up in the ICU. I spent the next year learning to walk again. I was standing a year later, when my son, at five, went through the same surgery my wife had to remove pre-cancer growths.

The public knew very little, with the exception of dark-hearted radio talk show hosts repeating – like a punch line – that I had shot myself. Yes, my near death was a joke to the people to whom I had stood up a year earlier on the issue of illegal immigration.

In 2010, I still polled highest in my party for the nomination, but my gut was unsettled. I was in a crisis of decision. I could tough it out, but I knew my family couldn't. Politically, the former and very popular Governor was running, and it was going to be uphill. My party's funders never respected my independence, which guaranteed a dirty primary. I could tough it out – I wanted to tough it out – but standing on the front porch dialing the reporter's office line, my heart was confirmed to announce I was passing.

Passing on my life dream.

This crisis was personal. It hurt on levels my ability to

write cannot grasp, yet I knew what I had to do. I was honest with the reporter. Credibility was not an issue because I was using the reporter's credibility, rather than a press release or a radio talk show. The reporter knew what I was doing, establishing the story with him first, and was using my credibility for higher placement of his story in the statewide newspaper.

I talked directly to the audience, not to political junkies. While I didn't detail the health issues or chronic pain, I did say it was best, right now, for my family; and I needed some privacy. We shared the values of suffering and loss of a dream.

* * *

Crisis management is a hard skill to master because we as leaders avoid crisis, which prevents us from practicing. But we do know this: The intensity of a crisis is personally one of the loneliest places on earth, and yet one of the noisiest, with people telling you what you should do.

Be honest. Be credible. Be your audience. Make an emotional connection.

STEP FIVE:

Be First to Frame your Narrative in Your Own Voice, with Facts and Sincerity

By Michael Steele, former Chairman, Republican National Committee and Lt. Governor, State of Maryland

The one thing you don't want in politics or business is to be unpleasantly surprised.

We pride ourselves on seeing every angle and knowing every pitfall; and when we don't or we can't, we hire consultants who supposedly do because there's nothing that will throw you off your game faster than the unknown.

So it was with particular attention to detail that my staff at the Republican National Committee (RNC) planned for me and over thirty members of the RNC's Site Selection Committee to visit the three cities in the final running to host the 2012 national convention.

It's no secret that my tenure as RNC Chairman had more than its share of unpleasant surprises. So my instruction to the staff regarding the site visits was simple: "lean, clean and *no* surprises!"

As the visits got underway, by any measure, they were going exceedingly well. These trips used to be about goodie bags and cocktail parties, but we had resolved to take a decidedly more business-oriented approach – with an emphasis on contracts, bus schedules, fundraising and hotel rooms; and as it turned out, the members preferred that (although they still wanted their cocktail parties).

But as they say, "the best laid plans..."

* * *

The day had already been long with meetings and tours with the Mayor of Salt Lake City, our respective legal teams and members of the Site Selection Committee. As this was the second of our three cities to visit, we had begun to establish a rhythm for the day; and by this point, it was definitely time for one of those cocktails. For most of that afternoon, I observed the courtesy of keeping my cell phone turned off. After all, if my chief of staff – or anyone else for that matter – needed to reach me, there were enough other cell phones nearby.

So when the executive director of the site selection committee, Belinda Cook, handed me the phone with a look of anger: "The office has been trying to reach you for the past hour; your cell is off" – I thought to myself: "Don't be mad at me; you told me to turn it off!"

But I would soon realize that she wasn't angry about the phone. Rather, a major conservative web site, the *Daily Caller,* wanted a "comment" on a story it was about to run that a member of the RNC finance staff had spent $2000 at a Los Angeles strip club that featured a sexual-bondage theme. And to make matters worse, the reporter was inferring that I was there.

I'll spare you the first words I uttered at that moment.

Needless to say, I realized that the countdown to the firestorm had begun; and I would need as many fire hoses as I could get my hands on.

There's nothing more revealing about your capacity to handle a crisis than the first steps taken after you realize you're in one – especially when you find yourself the central figure in a spectacle you had nothing to do with and knew nothing about (surprise!). So in my mind, there were three very necessary and important fire hoses to use:

1. Determine the facts;

2. Take the necessary steps to remedy or at least mitigate the damage done; and

3. Be the first to tell the story of what *really* happened.

I was confronted, however, with a twist: The staffer's night out on the town had occurred two months prior, but the *Daily Caller* was reporting the story as if it happened yesterday. And even though my office had provided the travel manifest that showed I was in Hawaii at the time, the story was written as if I had been the one stuffing G-strings with RNC donors' dollar bills.

Long before this crisis, members of my staff and I had been battling against an endless sea of anonymous mischaracterizations of our spending, broadsides against my leadership and an overall narrative set in motion by Establishment Republicans who just plain wanted me out of the job. So the thought that the Chairman of the RNC was spending donor money at a strip club was too sweet to just let run its course – they would be more than happy to help the story along.

To that end, it didn't take long for the flames of controversy to grow; and soon the phone calls from friends around the country, including a couple of Catholic bishops I know, let me know that this strip club narrative – whatever it was trying to become – must be stopped in its infancy. Framing the narrative or telling the story over the next 36 hours after the story hit the Internet would be critical if I were not only to survive this assault, but also to keep my reputation and dignity intact.

Failure not only to get in front of the crisis, but also failure to tell your story in your own voice, with facts, and most especially the truth, is the quickest way to accelerate a crisis and end any hope of surviving the noise. This is critical: **Be first to frame your narrative in your own voice, with facts and sincerity.**

One can get blindsided by the unexpected. But the trick is catching your breath and clearing your eyes soon enough thereafter to accurately understand the full depth of the situation and to answer all possible questions. It may not be easy as it sounds, of course; there's more to it than just getting out in front and saying this or that isn't true.

It's one thing for your actions or words to get you into trouble (trust me, I know a little about that too), but what do you do when your exposure comes not from something you said or did, but rather from what others have done, or from the efforts of those inside your organization to add fuel to the fire?

People often times overlook the fact that your problem is not necessarily one that is created by happenstance or even foot-in-mouth disease, but rather by the deliberate efforts of others to undermine you. In short, you can quickly find yourself having to navigate the rocky shores of the story now on the front page of the papers or trending on the Internet, but also having to put out the fires raging below deck that created the controversy in the first place.

The strip club story had such salacious appeal – a controversial CEO, sadomasochistic sex, misuse of the company credit card, questionable behavior by staff, the implications that the CEO was there or at least was aware of the bawdy night out –

like buckets of kerosene poured on a fire, the kind of misinformation that once it was out, just spread like wildfire. The perfect storm media crisis!

It's always easier to attract controversy with the right combination of elements. However, this type of crisis is not easy to fix because if you are in the middle of a raging fire and you turn on a water hose, you are not going to put out the fire; you may extinguish a few of the flames, but that's about it. So once the firestorm hits, it becomes a classic case of wisdom by hindsight: There should have been limits on the staff's use of credit cards; someone should have stopped the staff from going to the club, or at least asked where they were going, etc., etc.

But that's not realistic: Shit happens; and it especially happens when you are Chairman of the Republican National Committee. The actions of staff and personnel *will* percolate up to you, and you *will* get blamed for their mismanagement and even stupidity because the media *wants* to define you as the target, even as you are "managing" the situation.

It becomes important then to be the first to frame your own narrative (get in front of your crisis), in your own voice (you, not a spokesperson), with the facts (duh!) and with sincerity (please don't lie!). You are and should be the first storyteller – trying to control the narrative of a scandal, yes – but more importantly, being the first to define the narrative with the truth is a critical and essential element to be successful in managing the crisis.

My initial claims that I didn't know about the party at the strip club did not circle out much beyond the bubble of the RNC or Washington, D.C. for that matter. A lot of times the press grabs hold of (creates?) a narrative they like much better than the one you are giving them. Consequently, I had to deal with the reality that even when given the facts (for example, my travel manifest for that week) and the truth (really, I wasn't there!) – as a certain press outlet stressed to my communications shop – *the inference of my involvement* made for a better story.

So they kept perpetuating that narrative in every article, insinuating it, inferring it. The press, which I could barely get to acknowledge that I had a side to the story, found it easier to write that the Chairman of the RNC either knew about, condoned or participated in this activity (to further advance another narrative by some of the same GOP Establishment about spending at the RNC). Think about it: Writing that the "Chairman was unaware of the staff's activities as he hosted the RNC Members' Winter Meeting in Hawaii," or that "He immediately fired those responsible, and recouped the $2000 charged on the credit card," (both of which were true), makes for a much more boring narrative. But the truth usually does.

What you will quickly realize is that even after you lay bare the facts, the public may still not know or understand your "truth" because of how the press reports it. Therefore, you find yourself in my dilemma: I realized within a very short period of time after that phone call that no matter what I did, the press was going to write the story they wanted to write. No matter what I said publicly or my communications team provided privately, the press was not going to let the facts get in the way of a good "Washington Story."

So what's a scorched soul to do? What more could I do?

Not this. The typical reaction when confronted with the suddenness of revelation is to panic and then either to deny, deny, deny; and with each denial, sound more and more guilty of something.

Or to say absolutely nothing.

Thus it was for New York Congressman Charlie Rangel, when he found himself confronting allegations that he "improperly solicited donations for a public center and library bearing his name, and that he omitted hundreds of thousands of dollars of income and assets on disclosure statements."[23]

When the story about his questionable financial dealings were first reported by *The Washington Post* (which knows a good scandal when it sees one), with the brashness and bravado that only a New Yorker could muster, Mr. Rangel noted that "[f]irst of all, I normally advise people, as I have been advised, not to respond to these allegations that I abused my congressional discretion in writing on behalf of a school institution named after me because it would blow over; or, as more often I've advised members, that remember you don't have as much ink as the printers do." But then he declared, "So one of the things that I would use, hoping that it might catch on, is that I'm going to see how much damn ink *The Washington Post* has."[24]

Congressman Rangel decided against the say-nothing-at-all strategy and opted instead for the in-your-face-denial approach, by taunting *The Washington Post*.

Never a good idea.

You must remember, the press loves a challenge (remember Gary Hart?), and when a paper prints a story like this, it's never one and done. Always expect the reporter to have two, if not three, additional stories in her pocket. That's why it's important to get in front of the story with the facts and the truth, to be the storyteller.

First, YOU are showing your vulnerability, not the press; and the public appreciates it when you demonstrate that openness in the beginning of your woes: They have very little sympathy for it at the end. And second, it takes the steam out of the next article because that story will have to be about your facts.

But don't think you can shade the facts in any way – the press and your opponents *will* catch you in a lie. Just ask former Congressman Anthony "I can't say with certitude" Weiner.[25]

Needless to say, after *The Washington Post* deployed their ink, a congressional investigation was launched; and it led to Mr. Rangel being charged with 13 ethics violations, losing his committee chairmanship and being censured by the House of Representatives.

So much for getting in front of the story.

When first confronted with allegations of ethics violations, the Congressman misjudged his ability to manage the matter, leading him down the rabbit hole of bluster and denials. It became apparent that Rangel really didn't follow *any* advice, because his actions suggest he concluded just *being* the Chairman of powerful House Ways and Means Committee would somehow make him immune to scrutiny or criticism let alone censure.

While a title may lend itself to prestige, it carries with it the burden of transparency. Too many in public life forget that; and consequently, they expose themselves unnecessarily. When a reporter calls with the request to comment on a story they are about to print regarding your behavior or the behavior of others (that they believe you to be responsible for), catch your breath, clear your eyes and tell the truth – over and over again.

* * *

While people are generally familiar with the breathless denials and threats by public figures when caught in scandal, there have been a few in the not-as-public world of business who have also failed the most basic test of crisis management: Be the storyteller of your screw up.

Two examples of getting it right and getting it very wrong come to mind: the death of a Royal Caribbean Cruise passenger who fell overboard on his honeymoon in 2005, and the Carnival Cruise Lines *Costa Concordia* accident in 2012.

Big cruise lines deal with difficult stories and avert scandal every day, but when caught on the threshold of a perfect storm crisis, they often find it hard to avoid the temptation to ignore it, deny it or blame it on someone or something else. They tend to take to heart the advice of Charlie Rangel "not to respond to the allegations." But the loss of life or the image of a ship turned on its side makes it hard for them to say: "We have things under control." But some do try.

When the *Costa Concordia* sailed off its normal route and hit a rock off the coast of Giglio, Italy, the ship began to take on water. Its captain, Francesco Schettino, denied that the vessel had run aground, refused the help of coastal authorities, and then proceeded to sail the ship for another hour or so. The ship would eventually capsize, killing 32 passengers and crew. To make matters worse, Captain Schettino abandoned his ship with passengers still on board.

As if that weren't bad enough, *Costa Concordia* owners, Costa Cruises, offered "survivors of the deadly capsizing ship 30 percent off their next voyage."[26] Meanwhile, Carnival Corporation & PLC (the parent company) decided to apply the "Rangel Principle" and said absolutely nothing – for a long time.

Needless to say, the corporate non-response to the tragedy, along with the offer to take another cruise with them at a discount, effectively threw gallons of kerosene on the already raging firestorm around the ship's captain; and had the added result, much to the consternation of Carnival Corporation, of shifting the growing anger onto its CEO, Micky Arison and senior management. This had become the perfect storm; and the press had begun to add its own kerosene with the question "Where is Micky Arison?"[27]

This tragedy screamed for the personal touch of Mr. Arison: Having him on the scene, meeting with the press, speaking to the survivors and the relatives of the deceased, showing his personal compassion, all would have put him and Carnival Corporation in front of the story, especially with so many survivors ready to offer their account of what happened. His careful placement into the narrative would have made him the storyteller of this event, the first to frame the narrative of what happened; and more importantly, what would happen next to make things right. That way he would have taken responsibility, shown his humility and avoided being defensive when confronted by an increasingly agitated press corps.

But instead, the decision was made (probably by the

lawyers) to shut off communication and to have Carnival officials huddle amongst themselves, refusing even to talk to the families of deceased passengers. Consequently, the firestorm raged, and the credibility of both the company and management suffered irreparable harm.

* * *

When bridegroom George Smith went missing during his honeymoon aboard Royal Caribbean Cruise Line's *Brilliance of the Seas*, the only evidence that something had gone horribly wrong was a blood-covered metal overhang below Mr. Smith's stateroom. At sea, the ship's captain, Michael Lachtaridis, and his security team tended to Mrs. Smith, initiated a preliminary investigation of the events surrounding Mr. Smith's disappearance, and concluded that the death of Mr. Smith was an accident.[28]

However, Royal Caribbean also promptly reported the possibility of a missing guest to the Turkish authorities, the FBI and the U.S. Consulate. Once at port, the Turkish police, in cooperation with the FBI, conducted a complete forensic investigation onboard the ship. By immediately involving the appropriate authorities, Royal Caribbean began to position itself in front of a possible firestorm surrounding the mysterious disappearance and likely death of a passenger.

Moreover, as additional information was collected, the story gained widespread attention. As a result, the company created a blog to debunk "myths" about what happened aboard ship and about the actions of both cruise line personnel and Turkish police.[29] This form of inoculation was very important because it reframed the narrative around facts, and not speculation or outright lies. Even more impressive from a crisis avoidance perspective, Royal Caribbean International put its CEO Richard Fain on *Larry King Live*. Mr. Fain did not deny nor ignore the facts, but rather calmly provided a tick-tock of the events as he knew them.

Mr. Fain focused the discussion on what the investigation should be about ("I first of all agree with what Mrs. Smith has said at the very beginning. This ought to be about Mr. George Smith and his disappearance, and how we can get answers to that."); showed his compassion ("And I do understand: They [the Smith Family] have gone through a terrible trauma."); set the record straight ("But there has been so much misinformation: There have been so many erroneous, misleading, just dead wrong things said about this."); and offered an explanation for his company's actions ("We waited six months, and in deference to both the family and to the FBI's investigation we said absolutely nothing; we did as little as we could to do anything that would in any way impede the investigation or upset the family.")[30]

By initiating an investigation, taking charge of the scene until appropriate authorities arrived, and getting its narrative of the facts out front in a credible venue, Royal Caribbean averted what could have been a devastating firestorm. While not perfect, Royal Caribbean's actions serve as a good example of the importance of telling your story first and getting it right when you do.

* * *

Everyone believes there's a silver bullet in crisis management, but these are really 51-49 judgment calls. For the most part, we recognize the elements of a perfect storm crisis that make crisis management, at least in the short term, impossible. But when you are involved in a scandal that is all over the tabloids and given weight by the mainstream media, there's nothing you can do about that. No crisis manager in the world is going to prevent people from writing rumors or extrapolating from facts to create fiction, and putting their own desired narrative on your story way beyond what the facts are.

So what do you in a perfect storm when there is nothing you can do? In fact, the answer is not complicated or overly dramatic: Set your house in order and just keep telling the truth.

Don't let the storm put you into paralysis. Yes, you may be feeling as if nothing you say or do makes a difference. I know I did; long after the crisis was over the press was still writing the lies and exploiting the narrative. But at some point, I just had to say: "Screw it!" and fight back.

Even if it feels hopeless, you have to fight back.

And what does that mean? Every day, every hour, anything that is written or aired that is false or distorted, call the writer, producer or editor *directly* and get them to correct it. But know that is a constant fight – to get the truth in print or on the Internet; to get that letter to the editor printed, or the correction made, demands your utmost attention and effort. The principal here is accountability – yours and everyone else's; and at some point in time, believe it or not, the truth will catch up to those who perpetuate the storm.

As crisis guru Lanny Davis noted in his book *Crisis Tales,* in dealing with one of those storms, he got a necessary correction printed on a New Year's Day. While it was little read at the time, it was now in print and on the Internet, and he started to use that cite in every interview he gave, forcing hostile reporters off their narrative.[31]

Looking back on my own crisis, I certainly would have done a few things differently, starting with fighting back against the narrative that had been set in motion by the *Daily Caller*. If you want to wield the ultimate water hose against an emerging firestorm, you have to be a pain in the ass to the press until you make your point that the truth isn't what *they* say it is: It's what the *facts* tell us it is.

As much as the *Daily Caller* and others complicated my narrative with factual distortions, by not completing the basic steps of good crisis management – getting my story/the truth out front (check), in my own voice (check) and fighting back against repeated falsehoods and distortions (oops) – I allowed those falsehoods and distortions to take hold and spread. Even with notice before the printing of the story, I was caught behind the curve and mismanaged the one element that would have made a difference: Fighting back.

Lesson learned.

STEP SIX:

Develop a Clear, Concise Message, and Stick To It

By Steve Levy, former Suffolk County (NY) Executive

When an elected official is hit with a crisis, there are many ways to respond – some may resolve the situation; others may make it worse. At some point along the way, almost every elected official is going to face one type of crisis or another, whether it is on the governmental, political or personal level. When it happens, the press goes into a feeding frenzy.

It's always best to be prepared to deal with the situation in as organized a fashion as possible. Even though you can never predict when the crisis might come your way; you still can have in place a set of guidelines to live by, that can help you deal with the situation in the most effective manner possible.

A critical element of surviving crisis is to ***develop a clear, concise message, and stick to it***.

Of course, that's easier said than done. I had the unique perspective of being an elected official who was both a Democrat and a Republican, and who served as a county legislator, a New York State legislator and then as a County Executive (for the largest suburban county in the state, population 1.5 million). And let me tell you, there's no question that the scrutiny is greater upon executives – and in my neck of the woods, on Republicans.

When you're in office for 26 years as I was, there are many uneasy situations that will develop. You tend to learn as you go along. In some cases, my response was very effective; and in other cases, I made it worse.

Beware of Too Much Ad-libbing

Forming a consistent message is imperative in today's media. The attention span of the public and the press is much lower than it used to be. There is a dire need to stay focused and to envision the sound bite that you want to see in the paper the next day, which is why ad-libbing can often be a major mistake.

It is somewhat counterintuitive for people who go into public office to shy away from talking. It's in our DNA to want to get our point of view across and to engage in carefree banter with the reporter.

In my first few years as a county legislator, I would tell my secretary to put every reporter's call immediately through to me. I was anxious to hear what was on his or her mind and just as enthusiastic to give my two cents. I thought that this type of accessibility was also making me a "go-to guy" for the reporter.

There certainly is truth to the fact that reporters will reach out to those who are more accessible and likely to give a quote, especially if it's a spicy quote that has an edge, or is confrontational or controversial. But there is definitely a liability in being too quick to just speak off the cuff. Doing so can destroy the desired goal to stay concise and consistent.

We have to realize that a reporter is squeezed for space by his editors; and even though you may chat for half an hour, he is still likely to only use one or, at best, two sound bites from you. So, you'd better make it good, and you'd better not muddy the waters with so much extraneous information that you lose control over which sound bite will appear the next day (something I did quite often).

That is why, over time, I have learned to slow down and ask my secretary or aide to first squeeze out of the reporters what the topic was, and tell them that I would call back within 10 or 15 minutes. This would enable me to get my bearings and decide what I wanted to say. It was crucial in not only gathering the information that would bolster my argument, but it also would enable me to whittle down my quotes to as few words as possible. I even got to the point where I was writing down my sound bites before chatting with the reporter.

Often, I found it helpful to have a leisurely, off-the-record conversation with the reporter to give him background, but also to make sure I limited my blabbering once I was back on the record to just a few sound bites that were so crucial in getting my point across. Having the time to digest it helps you to remove extraneous verbiage.

Nothing kills a sound bite more than having too long a quote to get across your message. Again, these reporters are trying to shoehorn you into very small spaces within their article. Having that extra time can also help you contact allies whom you can line up to bolster your point of view and feed to the reporter.

A perfect example of how ad-libbing can hurt was seen in my reaction to the murder of an immigrant in Suffolk County.

I had been known as one of the country's foremost local officials in speaking out against the deleterious financial impact that illegal immigration was having on localities. In fact, I helped form an organization of mayors and executives for enforcement of our immigration laws. We had seen the impact that illegal immigration was having on our emergency rooms, schools, and law enforcement systems.

I had introduced legislation that required any contractor who wanted to obtain a contract from the county to first verify that they were not engaging in the illegal underground economy, thereby placing their competition at a disadvantage. We also implemented a policy that was a precursor to the federal Secure Communities Act, which forwarded to the federal government the names of individuals arrested in Suffolk County who were not here legally.

In any event, these proposals engendered a great deal of opposition from the illegal immigration lobbies and liberal pundits such as the editorial boards of *Newsday* and the *New York Times*. So when an Ecuadorian immigrant named Marcelo Lucero was viciously attacked and murdered on a street in Patchogue, New York one Saturday evening, the media sharks started to circle for lunch.

The more liberal elements of the media wanted to blame this murder on those who were opposing illegal immigration, claiming that our policies were fomenting a climate of hate which somehow led these perpetrators to kill this unsuspecting man who was simply and innocently walking down the street. Sent to cover the story was one of *Newsday's* most notorious "gotcha" reporters, Reid Epstein.

When the dastardly killing occurred, I knew from the start that this was going to be a firestorm, not only because of the savage nature of the crime, but also because it gave an excuse and a platform to the far left to try to fabricate dots between opposition to illegal immigration and violence, and then try to connect them. Some of my less experienced staff did not think it would be that much out of the ordinary when it came to the coverage. I knew better; there were radical elements salivating to prove their ridiculous points, that opposition to illegal immigration was bigoted and lent credence to the criminal elements the same way Bull Connor egged on mobs to lynch African Americans in the Deep South in the 1950s and 60s.

That's why we were so careful in tailoring our message early on to be short, concise and consistent. We wisely decided that I would not pick up the phone and speak extemporaneously; for fear that I would take the bait from a reporter such as Epstein, who was looking for the most volatile sound bite available to keep the story going. And for three days I did the right thing.

By the fourth day, Epstein had been pushing as to why I was not appearing at any memorials or giving further statements in the first few days of the aftermath. Well, first off, I thought that too early an appearance in such a volatile situation might politicize the event and take the focus away from the victim and his family, and place it instead on the controversies that related to Suffolk County policies on immigration. It's sad that one had to think this way, but I was absolutely correct in my analysis that that's what would have happened had I become overly involved.

There was also the concern that everyone in a crisis situation must consider – inadvertently creating the "YouTube moment." The press is just itching to get that one confrontational episode that will go viral. We wisely decided not to place ourselves in that position.

While I correctly stayed clear of a public gathering that could have turned into a spectacle, I made a huge mistake in taking the bait from Epstein's columns and calling him back on that fourth day. I thought that I could actually reason with him and tell him how deeply hurt I was by this senseless killing; and how Suffolk was going to do everything it could to bring justice to this victim and his family, and to punish those thugs who had perpetrated such a senseless act.

I recall the conversation quite clearly. I spent 30 minutes with Epstein pouring my heart out as to how horrendous it was that anyone could carry out such a cold-blooded attack. I expressed dismay that these young people had bragged about prior beatings as some kind of a sporting event. I chastised their peers within the school who knew about these attacks, yet failed to tell any authority figures – be they parents, police or teachers.

Had I hung up at that point, all would have been fine; but, as fate would have it, I hung on for one more question. And there it was: Epstein asked, with what sounded like a straight face, "So, why is that these types of events seem to only happen in Suffolk County?"

I responded: "Of course they do not. Hate crimes occur everywhere. Blacks are beaten in Boston. Gays are beaten in Texas. Jewish synagogues are desecrated in Nassau County. Whether it is New York City, Buffalo, St. Louis, or Tampa - no area is immune."

Yet, he asked again why it seemed to happen only in Suffolk County. I replied that they happen everywhere, but because of the debate that has inflamed the issue of immigration to such a high extent, the media goes into overdrive when such an event happens in Suffolk County. More specifically, I noted that while these crimes happen everywhere, in another county, it might just be covered as a one-day story hate crime. You wouldn't have all the side stories trying to link motive to county policy, I added. (Ultimately I was proven prophetic, in that this hate crime in Suffolk generated over 300 articles, while a similar hate crime murder of a Hispanic immigrant weeks later in Brooklyn received far less attention.)

That's all he needed to hear. It was a featured part of his story the next day. Nowhere was my 30 minutes of dismay about this senseless killing, or the fact that students had not reported these horrible events to authorities, or that we had to ensure swift and full justice. It was all about taking the one-day story out of context.

Epstein made it appear that my one-day story comment was my feeling of the killing itself. It's as though Epstein asked, "So what are your thoughts on Mr. Lucero's death?" to which I supposedly replied, "Had it been in another county, it would have been a one-day story."

Had that been how it actually unfolded, the criticism that followed would have indeed been justified. How could anyone so belittle the death of an innocent man by making such a comment? But that's not what I said.

Nevertheless, it was too late. There was no putting the genie back in the bottle. Once Epstein made it appear that this was the context in which I said it, all hell broke loose. Epstein's take on the conversation was extrapolated as fact by other reporters at *Newsday,* and, for that matter, reporters around the county, the state and the nation. A follow-up article in *Newsday's* "Spin Cycle" led with the headline: *"Levy on immigration killing: Just a one day story."*[32]

The fallout from the quote being taken out of context was startling. It now became a matter of fact in the *New York Times,* and even with human rights groups, that I had supposedly belittled this man's death. This simply wasn't true, but we felt I had to say something.

My gut instinct told me to keep pumping out the truth, in a clear concise way – that I was taken out of context, and that I thought this man's killing was horrific, and that it should not be linked to the illegal immigration controversy. But some staffers thought the horse had left the barn. No matter how much I protested, the fact that I would continue to protest in such a delicate situation would keep the spotlight on me rather than the healing that was so desperately needed.

It was decided that it would be best for me to take ownership of it and apologize. But apologize for what? I didn't think I did anything wrong. My comments were sincere and truthful. The one who should apologize was the reporter who took me out of context. But, it was thought that the constant finger pointing would look arrogant and narcissistic at that point. So, I wound up apologizing not for what I said, but for actually taking the bait and commenting at all over whether these types of crimes occurred in other places as well. By answering Epstein's loaded question, I created a distraction that the gotcha crowd was longing for.

To deal with this emerging crisis, I arranged a live, prime time, forty-minute speech to the public, via the local news channel. Had it provided closure on the controversy, it would have been worth it; but it didn't. The left wing was not about to relent on its attacks, while those on the right were scratching their heads wondering what the heck I was apologizing for. (While the liberal media abhorred my immigration stance; it was quite popular amongst the public at large.) This is a case in which the well-meaning apology backfired by taking me away from the clear, concise message that the crime was awful and should be prosecuted to the fullest extent of the law – and yet had nothing to do with a county law that required contractors to prove they are not hiring from the illegal underground economy.

Avoid that "YouTube Moment"

I noted earlier how in the aftermath of the Lucero killing that I sought to avoid the negative YouTube moment. Timing is everything in these situations.

Take for instance the aftermath of Superstorm Sandy. The time for elected officials to appear on the scene was immediately after the winds and rain subsided. Governors Chris Christie and Andrew Cuomo, along with President Barack Obama, toured the devastation, and placed their arms around the homeless and relatives of the dead while they were still in shock, aiming to lend a sense of comfort and a promise to help them through it. The President got a photo op, a bear hug from Christie and flew off to Vegas for a fundraiser. No flak; just praise from the media.[33]

Now contrast that to the awkward appearance of Mayor Michael Bloomberg a week later. By then, the lack of power, food and hope were building residents' frustrations to the boiling point. It made for one of the most cringing YouTube moments you'd ever witness. Bloomberg was verbally accosted by an angry group of residents who vented their frustration on him. He could only look down, say nothing, and take it – hoping his aides and bodyguards would usher him away from that spot.

At this point, the Mayor would have been much better served arranging a managed meeting with a handful of community leaders at an indoor setting, controlling who can get before the camera. He could have shown concern and leadership without making him look like the whipping boy. When you don't control the meeting, you may not control the message – the clear concise message you want to send – rather than becoming the subject of an embarrassing YouTube moment.

Some elected officials on Long Island suffered the same fate. After ten days without power, they went to a rally of residents furious at the Long Island Power Authority's (LIPA) lame response to the storm. The elected officials thought they'd score some political points taking the podium and bashing the utility. Instead, the angry residents, many whom hadn't had a hot shower in a week, booed them off the stage, wondering why these officials hadn't fixed this problem.[34]

Contrast that to the controlled press conferences Governor Cuomo held in his office, bashing the very authority that he oversees. Since LIPA was a state public utility, Cuomo was the most direct in line to be attacked; yet his media statements were made in managed settings and never allowed for the YouTube moment. He scored big in the subsequent polls.[35]

I faced a similar situation after a teenage girl was shot in the leg walking past a local elementary school in Huntington Station. For weeks, the locals were discussing whether to close the school. We were working hard behind the scenes on the problem, but knew an appearance at the school could indeed create a bad YouTube moment.

My staff and I had a big decision to make. If we didn't show, it might be taken as being apathetic. If we did, we knew we would be a lightning rod for anger. I wisely stayed away from the public forum. I would always be able to make up for it by having subsequent follow-ups with community leaders and announcing our progress.

But I tried to be too cute by half. I decided to show up after the meeting dispersed so I could mingle with the residents one on one and still ensure the public I was engaged.

Big mistake.

There's no such thing as one on one when you are the recognizable leader of the county. A group of four turned to eight, and then sixteen. Worse, a grandstanding legislator, who was still hovering around, charged over, and the shouting began. It was a tense moment picked up by a local reporter. But it could have been much worse. Thankfully, the television cameras were gone, or surely that footage would have defined the event and would have run over and over again. My subsequent meetings with community leaders at our respective offices went quite well, and we got back on track.

When a Rapid, Forceful Response Works (and When it Doesn't)

When a crisis hits, it's often difficult to figure out whether it's best to respond quickly and forcefully, as James Carville did so brilliantly in the first Clinton presidential campaign, or to just let the fire burn itself out without pouring on more fuel.

A rapid, forceful response could be effective in allowing you to control, or at least change, the narrative. In 2007, the New York State Assembly Hispanic Caucus threatened to withhold a *pro forma* extension of our county's sales tax unless I first agreed to support the construction of taxpayer-financed hiring halls for undocumented immigrants. I wasn't about to capitulate to such egregious blackmail, but toiled over whether we should quietly work out the issue through back channels, or face it head on and put my opponents on the defensive.

I chose the latter, and it worked. I held a press conference detailing all the senior, veterans, women and youth programs that would be gutted if the caucus had its way. We banged away with a clear, concise and consistent message. I changed the spin, put these legislators in the position of being blamed for hurting their constituency, and got them to back down.

In two other cases, my quick and forceful response served to make mountains out of molehills. In one case, an environmental extremist falsely claimed that I was raiding money from an open space fund to construct sewers for more affordable housing and to promote economic development. The claim was blatantly false – not a dime of open space money was targeted – and was barely covered by any legitimate media outlets. But I felt compelled to set the record straight and issued my own release countering that of the extremist.

Well, I not only succeeded in making it into a big story that everyone would read, but I wound up losing the spin as well. My third paragraph response didn't much offset a headline that read something like "*Levy accused of raiding water fund.*" In this case, my clear, concise response should have been nothing. Sometime letting a small fire just burn out on its own is better than pouring gasoline on it.

I made a similar mistake in responding to a blatantly political story floated by the Democratic majority of the county legislature that suggested I was allowing debt to balloon in Suffolk. I had earned a stellar reputation as a fiscal conservative, having presented eight straight budgets without a general fund property tax increase, while garnering seven straight bond rating upgrades. The opposition wanted to do something to put a dent in my armor, so they floated the debt story. And while it is true that the debt did climb, what was not mentioned was that the increased debt was due to 1) the construction of a state mandated new jail, which was passed in my predecessor's tenure, and which I sued to overturn; and 2) the fact that my vetoes of tens of millions of additional capital projects were consistently overridden by the same Democratic majority complaining about the debt they created.

I fought back with my own press conference, replete with charts, bells and whistles. Again, what was originally a small story limited to the county's official Democratic paper, had now gone mainstream, and I lost the spin once more. When the headline said, *"Levy answers claims of bloated debt,"* I knew I was on the defensive.

If You Respond, Win the Spin

Winning the spin is important, and keeping your message clear, consistent and concise is critical. Take for instance these two different potential headlines:

1. *"Suffolk college tuition to increase"*; and

2. *"Suffolk's proposed tuition increase slashed."*

In the case of one community college budget battle in Suffolk, both headlines would have been accurate, but the latter had a much better connotation for the county managers.

We had heard that the community college system's trustees submitted a proposal to sharply increase tuition. I fought it, and got the legislature to cut it significantly. Thus, while there was still an increase, it was much less than it would have been. We kept the media focus clearly and consistently on the trustees and their increase, while highlighting how we were the champions of more affordable education. We changed the narrative, got our supporters lined up to echo our elation of a job well done, won the spin, and managed to get the former, more complementary headline.

Contrast this to the government in one of the towns in Suffolk County. A newly elected supervisor proposed a whopping 68% property tax increase after campaigning as a tax cutter. While he presided over a very weak economy, he hadn't laid any foundation for this surprising and shocking announcement. Even though it eventually was pared down to about a 25% increase, it was too late: The damage was done.

When I came into office, I inherited a $238 million shortfall, but I had a bipartisan transition team that let the public know the size of the problem. It would be no surprise when a few months later we were cutting back on favored programs. As my budget came out, I made a list of who the press' "go-to" guys were and gave them a briefing. When a reporter eventually contacted them, the comments were predictably favorable. We won the spin by being prepared and delivering clear, concise points to our surrogates.

The bottom line is that you can't predict or control every crisis; instead, you can just try to be prepared to manage as well as possible if and when it hits. In some cases, you can let it die out with few ramifications, or change the narrative and win the spin. But there are cases where you will lose the spin, notwithstanding your best efforts and preparation.

Keep Moving Forward

So what do you do after you have taken a big hit? There are many possible answers to this, but one that seems most appropriate is to keep moving forward.

In 2010, I switched my party affiliation and sought the Republican nomination for Governor of the state of New York. The sole Long Island paper, which definitely leaned left, started to look at me quite differently, with much more aggressiveness.

In previous years as a Democratic executive, I had filed a New York State financial disclosure form – and no one seemed to care. But now, the newspaper and my partisan opposition (which fed off the inaccurate news stories) alleged that I had violated county law by filing the state – rather than the county – form. What they failed to consider was that I was required to file the state form because I was a member of a state commission; and that the state law was clear that once the state form was filed, there was no need to file a redundant local form (a fact that was confirmed by four of the state's leading ethics scholars, yet ignored by the "gotcha crowd").

Despite this hatchet job, I still left office in December 2011 popular in the polls. Afterwards, I conferred with friends in private sector marketing relations who urged me to let go of my innate desire to dwell and answer back. I just couldn't do it. Something within me was refusing to allow lies festering in the media to go unanswered. So I wrote my lengthy responses that few gave a darn about.[36] But at least it was cathartic.

I did, however, buy into their advice that moving forward with positive ventures is what will define you in the future. Bill Clinton could have faded away after his tenure and be remembered for testifying at a deposition about a blue dress. Instead, he led the charge to wipe out AIDS and malaria in the Third World, and he raised millions for victims of natural disasters worldwide. And then he goes off and becomes the wise elder statesman for his party; giving at the 2012 Democratic National Convention perhaps the most important game-changing speech one President ever gave for another.

Jimmy Carter, who left office after a stinging defeat, may go down as an ineffective and unpopular president; but he likely will also be remembered as perhaps the most charitable ex-President of them all, having been involved in Habitat for Humanity and other worthy causes. (If only he would stop meddling in US foreign policy!)

As far as second acts are concerned, perhaps none are as remarkable as Reverend Al Sharpton's. Here was a guy who had been complicit in exacerbating a false rape charge and defaming an innocent man, yet kept moving forward, and staying so relevant that he now hosts his own show on MSNBC and is an icon to the far left wing of the Democratic Party.

The guy who didn't move on, Richard Nixon, is still remembered almost totally for his last act, as he was leaving the White House in a helicopter prior to the expiration of his term.

The editor of this book, Jonathan Miller, sums it up wonderfully in the name of the Web site he founded, *The Recovering Politician.* Even though we are out of office, the policy wonk juices continue to flow. The best way to recover from being out of the limelight as a politician is to find a cause larger than you, and contribute toward it.

For me, it is my work with a group I co-founded, the Center for Cost Effective Government, a cadre of business and community leaders united to expose government waste and enhance consolidation and efficiency.[37] My last quote has yet to be given. The same could hold true for anyone in the private sector who was once in the limelight and is now in a different phase.

A crisis can seem like the end of the world when you are going through it. It indeed may be the end of *that* world, but as long as there are days ahead of you, there are new worlds to open up to. We are not just defined by the past. We are defined by the totality of our lives; and for most of us, there's still a lot of living left to do.

STEP SEVEN:

Own Your Mistakes, Take Responsibility and Sincerely Say "I'm Sorry"

By Rod Jetton, former Missouri State Speaker of the House

I will always savor the moment: proudly standing on a flower-covered dais in a packed, Missouri House chamber, with my right hand raised, repeating my oath of office. My wife held our Bible, and my loving family sat in the House well observing their dad, son and brother being sworn in as the second youngest Speaker in Missouri state history.

I certainly couldn't imagine that less than a decade later, I would be out of a job, have few friends, and be suffering in the midst of a gut-wrenching, career-ending scandal.

My predicament was largely my own doing. But it was taking responsibility for my mistakes that set me free.

* * *

Many wondered how a boy from a poor area like Marble Hill, Missouri could go from the lowest ranking member in the minority party to Speaker of the House in just four years. Some said it was my work ethic…and I did work hard. Some said it was my political skills…and I had been very successful at campaigning. Others said it was my friendly, likable style…and I have always made friends quickly.

But no one really seemed to know the real reason: term limits.

My House seat opened up only because my predecessor had termed out; and we had a chance to win the chamber majority only because so many Democrats were term limited. All of the senior state House Republicans had left office, giving a friendly, hardworking guy who knew how to raise money and help candidates win campaigns an excellent opportunity to be the Speaker in just two terms.

Life is always throwing opportunities your way, and I believe it's up to you to take advantage of them. I freely admit that the four years it took to win my first House campaign, re-draw the district lines, recruit candidates, win the majority and position myself to be unopposed for Speaker, were four of the busiest years of my life. I have never consistently worked that hard at anything in my life, and I thought I understood hard work.

Running track and setting school records required working out twice each day to get in the 100 weekly miles it took to win races. When I joined the Marine Corps, I learned a new level of hard work. They gave me 90 pounds of gear and ordered me to march through the hills, with no rest or sleep, through all kinds of weather, for days on end. Starting a small real estate business and making it profitable, took early mornings and stressful nights, day in and day out.

But all of those experiences were just preparing me for what it took physically, emotionally and mentally to recruit candidates, win the majority, unify caucus members, advance an agenda, get good press, and stroke donors – all while trying to be a good father, loving husband, and solid community leader back home and in the district.

Don't get me wrong: I am not complaining. The crazy thing is that I LOVED IT! I was having a blast; everything was going my way; everyone loved me, respected me, and wanted to know what I thought about matters great and small. The other positive aspect of all my success was the policy change I was able to implement. Expending political capital and pushing hard for the policies I believed in was never a question for me. I studied the rules, reached across the aisle to make friends and understood how to use my political clout to get things done.

In the House, it takes a united team to change things. Developing an agenda, unifying our caucus behind it, and leading them in the public debate was a very worthwhile experience that required using both the carrot and the stick. I rewarded both Democratic and Republican friends. I helped them with their priorities and gained their support on our agenda. But I also sometimes punished my opponents.

I made it clear that if you crossed my allies or me, there would be consequences. I removed chairmen, kicked members out of their offices, disregarded Senators' bills, and ignored the Governor's priorities, with no regard for party affiliation. In my mind, you were either helping my caucus pass our priorities, or you were slowing us down. It's amazing what can be accomplished in politics when a leader has more regard for results than positive public perception.

I take great pride in what we were able to do in Missouri. I'm pro-life; and we made it harder to get an abortion in Missouri, resulting in the lowest number of abortions performed since 1975. I'm also a gun nut; and after several failed attempts in previous years, we gave law-abiding citizens the right to carry. In 2003, Missouri had a $1 billion dollar deficit; but by the end of 2007, we had a $600 million dollar surplus. For the first time ever, we cut the size of our state work force by over 3000 employees. While our previous governor was forced to cut education funding because of the bleak budget situation, we were able to increase education funding by over $500 million dollars from 2005 to 2008.

Missouri also went from having the 47th worst roads in 2002 to the 9th best by 2007, resulting in 161 fewer deaths in 2006 – the biggest drop of any state in America that year. Missouri went from being the number one meth-producing state in the nation, with 2860 meth incidents in 2003, to just 1280 in 2006. That's a 55% drop, which made our state a safer place to raise children.

Hopefully, my liberal friends haven't stopped reading. We also increased funding for traditionally liberal programs such as autism support, S-CHIP's, Utilicare, First Steps, food pantries, Meals on Wheels, and drug courts. Ironically, these are the same programs that our Democratic Governor and his Democratic majority were forced to cut in 2001 and 2002 when Missouri was going broke.

Another exciting aspect to this story was that our budget improved, and we increased funding for education and other vital programs with no new taxes. In fact, we cut taxes. One of the few bills that I actually introduced and passed during my eight years was a tax cut on Social Security benefits. Because of state Senator Jeff Smith (*see his chapter, Step 2, above*), I had to compromise and put an income cap on it, but we still eliminated taxes for thousands of senior citizens in Missouri.

Now, I cannot take credit for all this success, nor do I want to leave you with the impression that I am solely responsible for all these changes. We had a unified team in the House helping me push this agenda and a Republican majority in the Senate, with Matt Blunt, a Republican, in the Governor's office. Strangely enough, it sometimes seemed like we had to fight our Governor and our Republican Senators more often than we had to fight our Democratic colleagues.

All in all, I think things are better in Missouri because of the changes we were able to make, and I am thankful to have played a small part in changing the direction of our state.

* * *

But there is a cost to everything. While I was successful in the political world, I failed in the personal part of my life.

For me, the costs were high. These successes led to my failure. Some of my choices negatively affected my family and friends and ultimately led to my political downfall. It's a sad story that I do not relish telling; but I hope by telling it, others can avoid the mistakes I made.

I enjoyed many successes, and success can be a wonderful thing; but if you're not careful, success can kill you. It sure took a toll on me. I tried to hide my vanity and pride; but deep down in my mind, I started to believe all the things lobbyists, Members, donors and conservative activists were saying about me. When you are a public official with authority over funding – and other Members' bills as well – folks tend to tell you what you want to hear. Everyone tells you what a good job you're doing, how smart you are, how thankful they are that you are in charge…or that nobody else has ever done, or could ever do, as well as you.

Of course in politics, not everyone is singing your praises. In Missouri, the *Kansas City Star* and *St. Louis Post-Dispatch* were not very friendly to a conservative Republican like myself. I received plenty of bad press. Liberals and those opposed to my agenda sent me thousands of emails and letters, which were sometimes plain mean.

Another item that made enemies and allowed the press to attack me involved my consulting company. In 2004, I had so many friends asking me to help them with their campaigns that I decided to start my own campaign consulting business. I didn't work for any House campaigns or the House Republican Campaign Committee that I controlled, but I helped some of my friends who wanted to move up to the state Senate or the U.S. Congress. I also was able to work on Mitt Romney's presidential race in 2008. Between my political activities, legislative duties and outspoken, tell-it-like-it-is attitude, I started picking up quite a few new enemies, and they never hesitated to start a nasty rumor or provide a negative quote about me when they could. Oddly enough, most of my attacks came from fellow Republicans.

You are probably asking why I didn't listen to my critics, or at least think about their charges. Well...people say such terrible things about politicians, and our motives are constantly mischaracterized, that we have to develop thick skins. For me, it was easy to chalk up all of the negative comments and criticism to enemy hacks that hated me, because I was either beating them in the legislative chess game or defeating them in a campaign. I told myself that no matter what I did, they would complain. My experience had shown me how easy it is for powerful leaders to listen to the flattery and discount the criticism when they are under fire.

Another negative consequence to the flattery and criticism a leader hears: They start putting everyone into two camps – You're either for them or you're against them; and if you're critiquing them or even questioning them, you must be against them. They become paranoid when friends or neutral folks, who are just being honest, try to tell them the truth. Unfortunately, I feel this sometimes happened to me and affected a few of my relationships.

But let's get back to the flattery. It slowly started affecting me. Not in the beginning – I understood what they were doing, and I told myself not to pay attention to them. But flattery has a way of slowly creeping up and changing your attitude – or at least it did with me.

Have you ever heard the story about the frog that was placed in the pot of boiling water and immediately jumped out and survived? If you have, then you know that same frog didn't fare so well when he was placed in some cold water and then the heat was slowly turned up until he was boiled to death and never even knew it. It's very embarrassing to admit that this happened to me. Looking back on my time in the legislature, I feel a bit like the frog that was slowly cooked to death and just didn't feel the heat rising. In fact, the warm water feels kind of good after awhile. But be careful, because the warm water will kill you.

What I needed was balance. Take a moment and think about the word: BALANCE.

It's a simple word that makes the whole world go round. Balance is required for the sun, moon, and stars to work like they do. It takes balance for us to walk, drive and function as human beings. Most importantly, it takes balance in your life to have healthy relationships with your wife, kids, family, friends, co-workers and fellow citizens.

The biggest mistake I made was not having balance in my life. I worked too hard at politics and forgot about my family, friends, community…and sometimes, the whole reason I went to Jefferson City in the first place. I remember telling my ex-wife that when the first campaign was over, I would be home more. Then the legislative session started – and I said that after session, I would be home more. Then I was gone working on redistricting, and when that was done, the next session started…and after that, I was working night and day to win the majority. I told her once we won the majority, I would be home more.

I didn't realize that winning the majority would take even more of my time, or that everyone would be depending on us, or that I would become even more entangled in my political life. The few times my wife complained, I thought she should have understood: I had more important things to do besides mow the grass, attend the kids' ball games, go to teacher conferences or hang out with her. I mean, we were trying to change the state, and I was making things better and passing all the issues we believed in. The fact is, I was working on good things, but she was all alone raising three kids who never saw their dad; and unfortunately, my actions proved that work was more important than them, no matter what I said.

There was nobody happier than I was when term limits ended my official position in 2008. I was tired of feeling responsible for all the problems that needed to be fixed in our state. I was also tired of getting beaten up in the press and having my enemies constantly trying to take me out. As a private citizen, I thought I would be able to be behind the scenes, work on my friends' campaigns and not be in the crosshairs each and every day.

* * *

Unfortunately, my marriage was in bad shape by that time; and even though I was out of office, things continued to get worse. In early 2009, we separated; and by October, we were divorced. I tried to tell everyone it was a good thing for me; but inside, it really messed me up. After all, we had been married almost 20 years and had raised three wonderful kids.

I was a 42-year-old successful divorced man, whose personal life was not turning out like he planned it. My dad was a Baptist preacher, and the best parents in the world had given me a perfect childhood. I was a family values conservative Republican who was not supposed to have these types of problems. I won't go into details, but my life was not reflecting the teaching my parents had taught me, nor was I being the example I wanted my kids to see.

I don't know if you believe in God or not, but I do! In December of 2009, God finally had enough of my hypocritical ways and got my attention. After spending the night with a lady I had reconnected with on Facebook, I was charged with felony assault. The press, along with my enemies, had a heyday. I immediately shut down my consulting business. Soon after that, I was notified that I was a target of a federal grand jury investigation surrounding my handling of a bill in the 2005 legislative session.

Needless to say, I started 2010 with no job, very few

friends and lots of time on my hands. As bad as my troubles were at the time, looking back now, I'm thankful for them. Life passes by so quickly, and very few of us get the chance to sit down and contemplate what is important. My troubles gave me a chance to analyze my weaknesses. With my pride stripped away, I was able to honestly evaluate my past actions. I saw how foolish I had been to put my family on the back burner. I learned how bitterness towards my enemies made me a bitter person toward everyone around me. The hardest thing for me to admit was that I wasn't the same friendly and caring guy who had gone to Jefferson City in 2000.

Most of my friends say, "Rod you were not that bad, you handled it well. You were polite and treated everyone with respect. We liked you then, and we like you now." I'm very thankful for those friends and their friendship, but I know the prideful thoughts I was thinking, and I know I should have handled things better.

As I mentioned earlier, I'm thankful for all the successes I was a part of. I'm also grateful for all the kind people I met along the way who helped and encouraged me. But I wish I would have worked less and stayed home more; been more forgiving and not gotten bitter at my opponents; been less prideful, less judgmental and more understanding. Plus, I wished I had lived the personal life I believed, instead of being such a hypocrite. Of course, I can't change the past. I can only look to the future and focus on learning from my mistakes.

Life is wonderful for me now. Each morning, I wake up and thank God for the day. I spend more time with my family and stay connected with my friends. I have a lovely new wife, a great job and a contentment I never knew in my first 42 years of life. I was never convicted in the assault case, and the grand jury suspended their investigation into the ethics allegation and never charged me with a crime. I have slowly begun gaining back the respect I lost from my bad choices, and I am even back in politics.

Let's face it. Sooner or later we are all going to make a mistake; we are all going to do something stupid that we regret.

Sometimes these mistakes go unnoticed and don't cause us much trouble publicly. But for those in the limelight, their mistakes are written about, analyzed and discussed in the public square.

It happens to celebrities, business leaders and athletes; but it also happens to parents, kids and everyday people. Anyone who has made a mistake that becomes public has a problem; and how you deal with it will either make it a bigger problem or put it in the rear view mirror.

Just in case you're thinking, *"It can't happen to me!"* think about this: Powerful politicians, corporate leaders, pro athletes and Hollywood stars all have opponents, enemies and even subordinates who believe it is in their best interest to help promote problems for them. The more powerful or well known you are, the more likely it is that others are looking harder to find the mistakes you make. Additionally, the press desperately needs scandals to generate readers/viewers, and most reporters dream each day about breaking the story that takes someone down.

* * *

So, when you've screwed up, it is essential to **own your mistakes, take responsibility, and sincerely say, "I'm sorry."**

Now admitting a mistake and saying sorry will not work in every situation. Ted Bundy wouldn't have swayed public opinion with a public apology. There has to be genuine remorse; and even more importantly, a change of behavior.

Mistakes typically fall into two categories:

1. Moral/ethical – These typically involve breaking laws, sexual exploits, or lying/fraud , etc.; and

2. Honest mistakes – These typically involve misstatements, misfiled paperwork, not paying taxes, etc.

Most people don't show up in the press or have a crisis unless they break a law. But powerful people, those who are leaders in the business world, sports world, or politics live with the reality that at anytime, even small mistakes can turn into full-blown scandals.

Having a mistake turn into a full-blown scandal can take several different paths, but it normally follows this seven-part process:

1. The mistake is made;

2. Someone finds out about it, rumors start;

3. Individual denies or ignores it;

4. It becomes a press story and won't go away;

5. A full scandal breaks out with calls for resignation/firing;

6. Individual apologizes for mistake and says, "I'm sorry"; and

7. One on one private follow up apologies to those involved.

Let's look at a few examples of individuals who made a mistake, took responsibility for it and apologized:

Michael Vick is a good example of someone who very publicly fell from grace. His interstate illegal dog fighting promotion did more than ruin his football career –it landed him in federal prison. To make matters even worse, he tested positive for marijuana in a random drug test while awaiting sentencing in federal court.

Vick instantly went from being one of the hottest stars in the NFL, with multi-million dollar endorsement deals, to a scorned thug whom the media lambasted for weeks and was hated by animal lovers everywhere. He went from making $25 million in 2006 and having endorsement contracts with companies including Nike, EA Sports, Coca-Cola, Powerade, Kraft and Rawlings – to losing his job, his endorsements, his houses, and ending up declaring bankruptcy.[38]

Shortly before his release from prison, Vick testified in his bankruptcy case that he intended to live a better life after prison. He said his crime was "heinous" and he felt "true remorse." On July 20, 2009, Vick was released from prison, and former Indianapolis Colts coach Tony Dungy spent time mentoring the quarterback. Most sports commentators thought the fan backlash would prohibit any NFL team from taking a chance on signing him to a contract; but on August 13, 2009, Vick signed a two-year, multi-million dollar contract with the Philadelphia Eagles.[39]

Vick eventually became the starting quarterback for the Eagles and made his fourth Pro Bowl in 2010. In 2011, the *Associated Press* and *Sporting News* named him the NFL Comeback Player of the Year; and the Eagles announced they had agreed on a 6-year, $100 million contract, with almost $40 million in guaranteed money. [40]

Since going through his troubles, Vick has been an outspoken critic of dog fighting; and he even lobbied for the passage of the Animal Fighting Spectator Prohibition Act, which would have established federal misdemeanor penalties for spectators of illegal animal fighting, and make it a felony for adults to bring children to fights. Additionally, in 2012, Vick became a dog owner again: After completing his parole, he was able to adopt a dog for his new family estate.[41]

Hugh Grant provides another positive example. The A-list

actor was arrested for a public act of indecency with a prostitute; a scandal that threatened his nice-guy image, as well as his high-profile relationship with actress Elizabeth Hurley.[42] But within a few days, Grant appeared on *The Tonight Show* with Jay Leno, apologized famously for doing a "bad thing"; an admission that crisis management types point to as the model for surviving scandal.[43]

A more cautionary tale can be found in the scandal that enveloped New York Congressman Anthony Weiner, when illicit pictures of him appeared on the Internet after he had been tweeting them to his followers on Twitter. Weiner's immediate response was to deny culpability. Once he was caught in the lie, he was soon forced out of office. Perhaps he'd still be a Congressman – or even the next Mayor of New York – if he had owned up to this relatively minor transgression immediately.[44]

* * *

My own mistakes ruined my reputation and ended my political career, but they also brought me to the realization that I had messed up and needed to genuinely apologize for my failure. Saying "I'm sorry" changed my life and helped me start down a path to regain the respect I had lost from family, friends and colleagues.

While my mistakes started as small issues that would not garner attention, they ended with a one night stand and assault charge that had to be dealt with immediately. The seven steps above can be applied to my story very easy:

1. I made the mistake;

2. The rumors got out;

3. I tried to ignore and deny it;

4. The assault charges made it public;

5. It quickly developed into a major scandal, and I had to shut down my business. I basically went into hiding and avoided contact with everyone as I dealt with the legal issues; and

6. I was candid about my mistakes and apologized.

For me, apologizing was easy; I knew I was wrong. Of course, an apology from a politician who got caught with his hand in the cookie jar didn't do much to take the heat off me. Nobody believed I meant it and it took time to prove my apology was genuine.

As with any mistake, there will be some who never forgive or forget it. But for me, accepting responsibility for my mistakes, apologizing, and changing my behavior, have allowed my life to return to normal and even repaired old friendships.

STEP EIGHT:

Present a Fix-it Plan

By Lisa Borders, former Atlanta Vice Mayor and City Council President

Sitting at my desk, head in hands, two words kept creeping into my brain:

Not again. O Lord, not again.

A few years earlier, in 2006, the city of Atlanta's former Mayor, Bill Campbell, had been convicted of three counts of tax evasion. He had been acquitted of the more serious charges of lining his pockets while serving as the thriving metropolis' chief executive during the boom years of the 1990s.[45]

Shortly after Campbell left office, ethics reform became the rallying cry in city politics; and our city council passed some of the most stringent ethics laws in the entire nation.

Now, as the Vice Mayor and City Council President, I knew that we were being held to a much higher standard. Not only would we be required to follow the strict new code; we would be expected to avoid even the slightest whiff of ethical impropriety.

But as I sat at my desk that fall day, I received information appearing to implicate a fellow City Councilperson in violation of our brand new code. The official was alleged to have conspired with a group of developers to inappropriately rezone real estate in the represented district.

Not again, I thought. Oh Lord, not again.

Unfortunately, the crisis crossed my desk long after I could have headed it off at the pass. I immediately called the accused Councilmember to gather all the facts. I knew it was critical to solicit all of the vantage points. But after multiple attempts, none of my calls were returned.

While I had nothing personally to do with the allegations in question; as Council President, I would be expected to take responsibility for fixing the problems at hand. I called the city's Board of Ethics, and its executive director was unsure if any law had been broken, or even if the Board had any jurisdiction. The ethics officer ultimately referred me to the County District Attorney for an "opinion" on the situation.

Without any notice to me or any members of the Council, the County District Attorney launched a full investigation. The DA then immediately hopped on the media circuit, transforming a murky private matter into a public scandal. The press, already sensitized to ethics issues from Mayor Campbell's term, seized on it with full force.

The circus was back in town.

A regularly scheduled council meeting intervened, and I had to preside. With the media looking for its pound of flesh, the issue naturally was raised.

The flame erupted. Now several members of the council were upset with *me* for how I handled the situation. I was admonished for not asking for their help, and not working harder to schedule a discussion with the affected member.

The crisis was painful and protracted. Fortunately, there were two happy endings:

First, the Councilmember accused of malfeasance was cleared of any wrongdoing.

Second, the resolution of the experience taught me a very valuable lesson about crisis management: **Gather the affected parties and present a fix-it plan.**

Once the heat of the argument dissipated, my fellow Councilmembers and I developed a concrete plan for action and communication going forward. The accused member agreed to return my phone calls promptly – as well as those of fellow councilmembers – particularly in times of crisis. I agreed to consult with my colleagues immediately when a matter this sensitive was brought to my attention, before it garnered public notice. And going forward, this problem-solving strategy was employed successfully in numerous situations.

* * *

Of course, I was not the first public official who had inherited a scandal that was entirely not of her own making. Every day indeed, elected officials – particularly those in executive positions such as mayor, governor, President – deal with crises caused by colleagues or underlings who have not applied the same rigorous ethical and legal standards that the executive employed for herself.

Worse yet are the crises that come completely out of the blue and are the result of forces of nature: explosions, snowstorms, and natural disasters. The same rule of crisis management that I learned applies to these cases as well – gather your advisers and colleagues close, and develop and present a fix-it plan to your stakeholders. Failure to do so can transform a small crisis into a reputation-destroying catastrophe.

Take two contrasting examples from the world's largest stage – recent presidential reactions to enormous natural disasters. After Hurricane Katrina ravaged the Gulf Coast, George W. Bush's failure to present a decisive fix-it plan – he famously was pictured watching the damage from the secure distance of an airplane,[46] and was quoted praising his notoriously ineffective FEMA chief ("Heckuva a job, Brownie")[47] – led his popularity ratings on a precipitous nose dive.

Barack Obama learned that lesson well; and when Hurricane Sandy inflicted great damage to the East Coast, Obama sprung into immediate action, reaching across the aisle to New Jersey's Republican Governor Chris Christie to offer immediate, personal help, and develop a plan to remediate the damage.[48] Many credit President Obama's response to the widening of his victory margin in his re-election campaign a few days later.

Other Presidents' failures to present adequate fix-it plans have been blamed for their subsequent political defeats. When George H.W. Bush failed to offer a sufficient economic plan to deal with the struggling American economy, Bill Clinton seized on Bush's neglect, focused his campaign efforts on "It's the economy, stupid," and defeated the incumbent, who months earlier had stratospheric approval ratings, stemming from the successful Persian Gulf conflict. Similarly, Jimmy Carter's inability to present an adequate plan to resolve the Iranian hostage crisis projected a weakened presidency among the American people, enabling Ronald Reagan to surge into office on a platform of restoring national greatness and global supremacy.

Politicians aren't the only chief executives who'd be wise to develop a fix-it plan to survive crisis. The classic corporate crisis management success story can be found in Johnson and Johnson's efforts to deal with its Tylenol poison scare. In 1982, seven people died after taking Extra-Strength Tylenol capsules that were bought off store shelves in Chicago. As concerned Americans became frightened about becoming the next victim of the terroristic activity, Tylenol's market share plunged nationally from 37 percent to 7 percent.

Johnson and Johnson sprung to action quickly, and immediately presented and enacted a fix-it plan, recalling 31 million bottles of the product, at a cost to the company of more than $100 million. Soon thereafter, Tylenol products were reintroduced to the market with triple-sealed packaging and discounted pricing, and over 2000 salespeople were sent across the country to assure a wary public. The company completely rebounded and survived what could have been an existential crisis with boosted sales and an even more pristine reputation.[49]

Contrast that with Exxon's response a few years later when its oil tanker, the *Exxon Valdez*, spilled more than 11 million gallons of oil into Alaska's Prince William Sound. Exxon waited ten days to respond publicly, and its chief executive did not visit the region for two weeks. Meanwhile, its flacks mostly responded with "no comments," and the company refused to take responsibility for a problem of its own employees' making. Contrast that with Johnson and Johnson, which took responsibility for actions *completely out of its control*. The *Valdez* scandal has forever sealed Exxon's reputation as an opponent of environmental protection.[50]

Have you ever heard of Friendster? Probably not. It was the original social media experiment that took the nation's young people by storm. However, when its technological capacity could not meet customer demand, and no fix-it plan was put into place; the company, once valued over $1 billion, nearly disappeared from the nation's attention.[51] Its much younger competitor, Facebook, learned the lessons well from the Friendster disaster; and for every crisis the company has endured – from unpopular new features to controversial privacy settings – Facebook has met the concerns with prompt and public remedial action.[52]

You needn't be a high ranking politico or a Fortune 500 titan to profit from the lesson of presenting a fix-it plan in a time of crisis. It's a simple and obvious human response to crisis. Whether there's a problem in a business dealing or a personal relationship, the party that quickly offers an immediate plan to resolve the crisis or to fix the problem often will see her professional or personal goals realized. Take note errant spouses: When you screw up, saying sorry might not be sufficient – offering a coherent and responsive plan to ensure that you don't make that mistake again is the best recipe for marital happiness.

Don't just take it from me: Look to the Good Book, however you define it. Nearly every world religious tradition has as a central principle the notion that offering a fix-it plan is critical to being a good moral actor. In my own religious tradition, Christianity, the Old Testament story of Jonah and the whale is instructive: God only forgives the people of the sinful Nineveh when they change their behavior for the better.

Indeed, our system of government can learn the same valuable lesson. A few years ago, I co-founded (with this book's editor, Jonathan Miller, and others) an organization called No Labels, which involves hundreds of thousands of Americans who believe that our leaders should put aside hyper-partisanship in favor of bi-partisan problem-solving. But unlike most screaming heads in the polarized news media who identify problems without solutions, No Labels offers a concrete fix-it plan to cure our democracy's ills.

For example, in order to ensure that the incentive system in Washington is changed to promote action instead of paralysis, No Labels has offered a plan called "Make Congress Work." The plan offers...you guessed it...*twelve steps* to enable recovery of our broken politics[53]:

1. No Budget, No Pay – If Congress can't pass a budget on time, it shouldn't get paid.

2. Up or Down Votes on Presidential Appointments – All Presidential nominations would get an up or down vote within 90 days.

3. Fix the Filibuster – Require real (not virtual) filibusters and end filibusters on motions to proceed.

4. Empower the Sensible Majority – Allow a bipartisan majority of members to override a

leader or committee chair's refusal to bring a bill to the floor.

5. Make Members Come to Work – Make Congress work on coordinated schedules with three five-day workweeks in DC and one week in their home district.

6. Question Time for the President – Provide a monthly forum for Members of Congress to ask the President questions, to force leaders to debate one another and defend their ideas.

7. Fiscal Report to Congress – A non-partisan leader should deliver an annual televised fiscal update to a joint session of Congress to ensure that everyone is working from the same set of facts.

8. No Pledge but the Oath of Office – Members should make no pledge but to the flag and to the Constitution.

9. Monthly Bipartisan Gatherings – The House and Senate should institute monthly, bi-partisan, off-the-record gatherings to get members talking across party lines.

10. Bipartisan Seating – At all joint meetings and sessions of Congress, each member should be seated next to at least one member of the other party.

11. Bipartisan Leadership Committee – Congressional party leaders should form a bipartisan leadership committee to discuss legislative agendas and substantive solutions.

12. No Negative Campaigns Against Incumbents –

Incumbents from one party should not conduct negative campaigns against sitting members of the opposite party.

The No Labels' Make Congress Work plan seems like simple common sense. But common sense fix-it plans are simply what's missing from today's politics.

* * *

So if you've made a mistake – or find yourself being held accountable for the mistakes of others, or for outside forces that have laid the buck on your desk – here's some simple, common sense advice on constructing the appropriate fix-it plan:

- **<u>Gather your team quickly</u>**: Make sure you surround yourself with the top decision-makers and administrators in your organization. If the circumstances warrant, and if you can afford it, be sure to include an attorney and/or a crisis management expert who can help you navigate through the most complex legal challenges.

- **<u>Develop a proportional solution</u>**: Gauge as best you can the size of the problem; and with your team, develop a remedial plan that proportionately addresses it. Don't overreact – Tylenol didn't give away millions of free bottles of their product – but most of all; don't underperform: The plan has to be large enough to address the issue it is helping resolve.

- **<u>Get the fix-it plan out quickly</u>**: The more days you wait without a remedial response, the more ill will you will accumulate. Understand that no solution is perfect; so err on the side of a speedy response to ensure that your stakeholders understand your concern and empathy.

- **Show tangible sacrifice**: Even if the problem wasn't your doing, demonstrating your own sacrifice will help pacify your stakeholders. Consider Barack Obama's 2013 decision to take a 5% pay cut in solidarity with federal workers who were being furloughed, even though in his opinion (and mine), the government sequestration cuts were not all his doing.[54]

- **Take visible actions of charity and compassion**: There is no more powerful image than a senior government or corporate official personally visiting communities affected by crisis, and lending a physical hand or a personal show of support to those who are working on the problem. George W. Bush's greatest moment may have been standing at Ground Zero of the World Trade Center, applauding the law enforcement officials who'd been the heroes of 9/11. Get your clothes dirty, your shoes muddy, and demonstrate that you understand that all humans are equal, no matter the position they hold.

We all make mistakes. But it's been a consistent theme of human history that the most successful individuals are those who clean up their errors and implement a fix-it plan of action. It's not only the right thing to do, but it's also the right thing to enable you to survive your crisis.

STEP NINE:

Listen to the People You Trust and Ignore All Others

By Jimmy Dahroug, former Democratic nominee for the New York State Senate

"You're going to lose this primary. You need to throw a Hail Mary pass!"

A friend and mentor, whose political instincts I value highly, was looking out for me. He simply did not trust my election strategy. And it seemed like everyone, including friends and family members, agreed with him.

I didn't listen to any of them. Only to the man I had hired to advise my campaign.

And I won.

* * *

Politics is, if anything, personal. So when it comes to campaigns, almost everyone thinks they've got expert advice. The truth is that while people in your lives have good intentions, they often do not know the best course of action. It's *your* good name that's on the line, not your advisers', family members', or friends'. *You're* the one who must accept the outcome of the election. And no matter how the campaign or crisis ends, *you* want to know you took the advice you trusted the best.

Above all, **listen to the people whose advice you trust, and ignore all others.**

So how do you decide whose advice to take in your particular circumstances? It comes down to a few basic steps – whether in politics, business, or life:

1. Do your homework to assess your needs;

2. Choose an expert in the area *specific* to your needs;

3. Make sure you're comfortable with the expert and their specific advice;

4. Do a final gut-check before committing to a course of action; and

5. Once you're committed to your decision, decline the advice of others (no matter how well meaning they are).

A critical period of my state Senate campaign in 2006 illustrates each one of these steps. In my case, holding my fire – despite nearly everyone telling me to attack – was one of the toughest things I've ever had to do.

* * *

In a Democratic primary for the New York State Senate, I was running against a well-funded businessman as well as a legislator who represented my hometown, the Democratic base of the district. And at the ripe old age of 27, I had the smallest amount of funding and resources.

My strategist, Mike Dawidziak, devised a mail plan targeting likely Democratic primary voters. For Mike's plan to work, I had to save my limited cash, let my opponents underestimate me, and send mailings in the final week of the primary – just after Labor Day, when the bulk of primary voters would be paying the most attention. As Mike was fond of saying: "Don't fire until you see the whites in their eyes."

My opponents were bombarding mailboxes with ads much earlier in the summer. I only had the funds for three, maybe four mailings. Mike warned me that resisting the urge to send mailings while my opponents were firing away would be incredibly challenging.

Mike's prediction was right on the money. My supporters began growing concerned, as their mailboxes filled with ads for the other candidates. They urged me to start mailing. Regular volunteers would ask "How 'bout just *one* mailing... just one?"

I cannot overstate the negative feedback. My own mother thought I was going to lose! She wanted to believe me when I told her we had a plan, but how could she? My mother saw the mail pieces coming from my opponents and nothing from me – day after day. How could she not have her doubts?

The absence of mailings also fed into the perception that I didn't have the funds to win, which made the pressure even more intense. After all, I was a "27 year-old *kid,*" as my critics would taunt, running against an experienced legislator and a wealthy self-funding businessman. Weeks without mailings added fuel to critics who argued, "See, he just doesn't have the resources." Even dedicated supporters must have had their doubts about my ability to pay for an adequate mail plan. Some would email me links to anonymous blog posts predicting a terrible loss, or counting the days that went by without a mailing from me. The pressure was excruciating.

When they failed to convince me to spend my mailer budget early, some of my friends and supporters suggested that I attack my primary opponents in the press, to at least get some free publicity. But any engagement would undermine our strategy: We wanted my opponents to underestimate me until our mailings hit, and when it would be too late for them to respond. We couldn't do anything to get their attention turned on me.

There were times when I had my own doubts. It's almost impossible to face that much negative feedback from people who believe in you – who are sincere in their support – and not second-guess your plan of action. When I thought things over and considered my options, the stealth strategy was the only approach that made the most sense. There were no guarantees, but it met every one of my criteria for deciding; and that helped me stay resolute.

The final week of the campaign finally arrived – and so did my mailings. I was able to raise enough funds for four well-designed mail pieces. They hit voter mailboxes in consecutive days leading right up to primary day. The sense of panic from my supporters turned to cautious hope. The cocky verbal barbs they'd received from supporters of the other candidates began to subside. Suddenly, it was the other side panicking.

In the end, our approach proved victorious; and it wouldn't have happened if I listened to the advice of others. Even the naysayers ultimately admitted my strategy was the correct approach, and that I was right not to listen to them.

* * *

How did I know to take the advice of Mike Dawidziak, a strategist I had known for only a few months, who worked primarily for clients in the other party? It really came down to his expertise in that specific area, his solid track record in campaign strategy.

Several local elected officials who had suggested that I should change course had won general elections in overlapping parts of my district. But remember: Advice that fits your specific needs is paramount, and I needed advice on campaign mail strategy for a *primary*, not November.

There were other factors that played into my decision: comfort level and instincts. I refer to "comfort level" in its broadest sense: Dawidziak stood by his advice, explained it well, and defended it without being defensive. He wasn't pushy. Instead, he was patient and allowed me to ask questions, kick the tires of the strategy, and run through "what if" scenarios.

I also came to learn that instincts matter. Instincts, of course, are intangible, and they are different for everyone. For me, if something is wrong, I'll experience a nagging feeling in my gut. I don't mean butterflies or nervousness about whether a plan will work out: I just mean a basic gut feeling.

To be clear, I'm not advocating an approach that's entirely based on instinct. With Mike's mail plan strategy, I first considered it rationally, and it made sense. As I explained earlier, I explored all angles, and Mike answered my questions to my satisfaction. But there was something else – the plan checked out with my gut. It "felt" right – or at least it didn't "feel" wrong.

I listened to the people whose advice I trusted, and ignored all others.

And I won.

* * *

There are plenty of examples in politics that demonstrate the importance of following this crisis management strategy. Indeed, Jerry Brown's 2010 gubernatorial campaign in California resembled mine, just on a far, far larger scale.

Former Amazon.com CEO Meg Whitman, Brown's general election opponent, was a billionaire with a seemingly endless supply of cash to blanket California's airwaves with campaign ads. There was no way Brown could match Whitman's ad buys throughout the race. His best hope was to save his funds until the homestretch when voters were paying the most attention, and when his ads would count the most.

Not only did Brown receive negative feedback along the way – the criticism blanketed the airwaves. The candidate had to remain calm and resolute, as reporters asked him about anonymous sources within his own party that questioned the wait-until-the-homestretch strategy. The open criticism fed into the unfair perception that Brown was too old and didn't have the energy to run. It also had the potential to dampen the enthusiasm of donors from giving all they could; and Brown needed every bit of funding he could get against Meg Whitman's mega-millions.

As difficult as it was, Brown had no choice if he wanted to win. Blowing his cash early would likely ruin his chances. Brown simply had to stay strong and respond to criticism by repeating his confidence in his strategy. In the end, he won that race. But he probably would have had no chance if he buckled under pressure from critics.[55]

Barack Obama would not have been elected to the U.S. Senate, and ultimately the White House, without a similar approach. As an obscure state senator in Illinois, Obama ran in the 2004 Democratic primary for the U.S. Senate against two more highly favored opponents: State Comptroller Dan Hynes and wealthy businessman Blair Hull. Obama's strategist, David Axelrod, gave him the same strategic advice Dawidziak gave me: Save your funds until the end; let your opponents focus on each other and dismiss you until the homestretch, when it's too late.

Barack Obama held his fire. As he wrote in his memoir, *The Audacity of Hope*, Obama believed in Axelrod's approach; but it was painful driving down the street and seeing Blair Hull's signs put up by paid crews with unbelievable efficiency. Hull had blanketed the airwaves with TV ads six months before primary day. He was everywhere, and Obama received panicky calls from supporters urging him to spend his money on TV ads immediately. As challenging as it was, Obama knew he had to trust Axelrod and hold his fire.[56]

Assembling an expert group of advisers, and trusting

their counsel, is a wise strategy in any arena. Even in the world's most intense. Take Bill Clinton. During his rocky first two years in the White House, the President relied primarily on aides from his time in Arkansas and his presidential campaign. He began to understand that loyalty was important, but not sufficient; he needed advisers with more experience navigating through the difficult Washington Establishment.

The defeat of his health care initiative and the 1994 GOP takeover of Congress gave Clinton a wake up call. He brought in new advisers to work with his team. They had more experience with Washington leaders, and some had worked for prominent Republicans. It frustrated longer serving members of his staff, as there were times when Clinton chose controversial ideas from advisers who worked primarily for the other party. But it didn't matter to Clinton where the idea came from; after considering all of the angles, Clinton trusted his gut, and listened to the experts he had carefully selected. And as a result, the Big Dog was re-elected with an overwhelming Electoral College majority.

Listening blindly to your advisers, and failing to trust your gut, however, can prove calamitous. Ask Rick Lazio, my childhood Congressman. A telegenic, well-spoken politician, Lazio had long been watched as a rising star. But he'll always be remembered for a moment in his U.S. Senate race against Hillary Clinton: a televised debate in which he "invaded" Hillary's "space" and turned off viewers and voters.

Lazio had hired Mike Murphy, a high profile and nationally respected consultant. Murphy advised Lazio to use the debate to push forward a campaign finance agreement he was asking Clinton to sign. Murphy argued that there was no way Lazio could be "too aggressive."

The advice turned out to be disastrous. In later interviews, Lazio explained that he had a nagging feeling in his gut. Lazio appreciated that Murphy was advising what he thought was best, and he respected Murphy's track record; but Lazio knew he should have trusted his own instincts. To this day, Lazio advises using consultants, with one caveat: If the advice doesn't square with your gut, just don't take it.[57]

* * *

The lessons outlined in this chapter are almost universal. For example, if your business is suffering from a public relations crisis, you'll probably be bombarded with suggestions from well-intentioned colleagues, friends and family. You'll also likely be exhausted from the stress. Use this approach to keep yourself grounded and focused.

We rely on advisers in part because they specialize in areas where, practically, we do not have the time to study in-depth. But the job is not handed off entirely to the adviser; the principal still has a central role to play. We are the ones who know our own unique needs and circumstances the best. They are the advisers, but it is *our* job to manage the advising process; and ultimately, it is *our* decision to make.

As a result, it is critical that you do your part. That means learning about the area in which you need advice. This research can come in many forms: reading up on cases similar to yours, speaking to people who have been in your situation or speaking to potential advisers on an exploratory basis. This will provide some foundation for knowledge, so that you're not flying blind.

I'm not suggesting you become the equivalent of a hypochondriac patient who drives his doctor nuts after reading WebMD. An example of a happy medium is the informed car buyer who takes time to read about her options in *Consumer Reports*. When exercised reasonably, more informed questions serve to help the adviser-client process. You each raise each other's game in order to find an effective strategy for your needs. Informed questions lead to informed decisions.

After you've done your homework, ask these guiding questions when evaluating advice: Does the advice fit the circumstances adequately? Are the people offering it experts in their field? Remember to be specific: Have they dealt with these specific types of crises before? (For example, your vice president for marketing likely does not have the track record or expertise as a crisis communications consultant.)

If they've passed the smell test so far, don't let up just yet. Make sure the adviser respects you and your situation. Although crisis consultants may be well suited to address your business's needs, are they really trying to understand your unique situation? Are they really listening to you and critically thinking to apply their knowledge to help solve your problem? Or are they reciting cookie-cutter, one-size-fits-all strategies? Doing your homework also helps you evaluate the answers your adviser or potential adviser gives you in this stage.

Within reason, the adviser should be able to answer your questions and explain what happens with the endgame in different scenarios. To be clear, this doesn't mean the adviser should overpromise or guarantee what cannot be guaranteed. In my case, Mike Dawidziak would not overstate my chances of winning: He was honest – there were no guarantees (there rarely are). But in my case, or in the case of a business owner, it is far better to trust a counsellor who tells you what you need to know, rather than what you want to hear.

It is also okay to consider advice from others before you make your decision. Friends can be great sounding boards, and they may have some good ideas. But once you decide you're confident you've found the right choice, don't allow others to mess with your head. They almost certainly mean well, but you're the one who must live with the consequences.

Remember your final gut-check. You know yourself and your situation better than anyone. If you've got a nagging feeling that an approach isn't right, your instincts may be right. An adviser or friend can disagree – they can argue passionately – but they need to respect that at the end of the day it's your decision. Remember Rick Lazio's mistake – no matter how prominent the adviser is, don't discount your own judgment.

STEP TEN:

Don't Bear Grudges; Yesterday's Enemy Can Be Tomorrow's Ally

By Loranne Ausley, former Florida State Representative

Partisan politics can often resemble war.

Opponents stake themselves on opposite sides of an issue, a race or each other; and soon enough, one side claims victory and the other side defeat. But what happens after the political "battle" showcases the very nature of your personal character, physical wellbeing and lasting reputation as a politician?

There is a critical lesson to be learned: **Don't bear grudges; yesterday's enemy can be tomorrow's ally.**

* * *

My path to politics was never straight and deliberate, but rather meandering and inevitable, as I grew up in a small North Florida town that also happened to be the capital city. My grandfather was a former state senator, mayor and trusted adviser to Florida governors in the early 20th century, and my father was the proverbial apple that did not fall far from the tree. As a result, the discussion of politics was a regular and natural occurrence at my family's dinner table. My father's political acumen was honed at the side of Florida's great civil rights leader, Governor LeRoy Collins, and through his many years of voluntary service in state and national politics.

My first real experience with the political process took place in 1974 when I was 11 years old. My father decided to run for a Florida Senate seat that spanned 12 North Florida counties, stretching more than 300 miles across the deep rural panhandle. Every Saturday, my family and our supporters decorated our trucks and station wagons with campaign signs, loaded up our family and friends, and headed towards the nearest parade, festival or fish fry, often hitting 5 or 6 events a day. I have fond memories of these "motorcade Saturdays," when we would stop and visit in every little town along the way.

My dad ran a great race but ultimately lost in a runoff to a sitting House Member from a neighboring rural county. I recall how everyone around him (including his 11 year old daughter) felt defeated and devastated, yet he handled this loss with such grace. My dad's political career didn't end with that loss. He went on to a brilliant career in law and banking and served governors and Presidents for many years. My father is still considered one of Florida's most respected political advisers.

While this experience might have turned many away from the political arena, that was not the case for me. Watching my dad's grace in the face of defeat became my first, and most important, lesson in politics and life: *recognizing victory even in defeat.*

Something about that early campaign experience drew me back into the political arena – and after college I landed my first "real job": as a field organizer with Bob Graham's campaign for the United States Senate. This was my first taste of a statewide campaign. Bob Graham had been one of Florida's most respected governors for 8 years, and his 1986 campaign victory over incumbent Paula Hawkins sent him to Washington as one of the "freshmen to watch." I moved to Washington and experienced Capitol Hill as a low-level staffer in Graham's Senate office before heading off to law school.

After two years as a litigation associate at a large Miami law firm, it was hard to resist the opportunity to return to the political world – particularly in 1992, with the excitement surrounding the rising Democratic star, Bill Clinton. Fast forward through a fundraising position on the Clinton campaign, and a variety of mid-level positions in the Administration, and the next thing you know, I was back in Tallahassee serving as the chief of staff to Florida's Lt. Governor Buddy MacKay.

In 1990, Buddy MacKay and Lawton Chiles formed Florida's "dream team" to unseat the incumbent Republican Governor Bob Martinez. Four years later, Chiles and MacKay won a close re-election against challenger Jeb Bush. Throughout their eight years governing together, Chiles and MacKay formed a strong team. Governor Chiles entrusted his Lieutenant Governor and good friend with many of his key legislative and policy priorities. When I returned to Tallahassee, MacKay was already facing a tough gubernatorial campaign against a revived Jeb Bush.

I settled quickly into state politics – learning the importance of navigating the dance between the executive and legislative branches. As a lifelong Democrat, it was discouraging to watch as the Republican Party swiftly took over one legislative chamber, then the other; as Florida became the first southern state to experience the Republican wave. Buddy MacKay's impeccable political resumé, and his earnest service as a legislator, Member of Congress and a loyal Lt. Governor, were not enough to stem the Republican juggernaut.

In a cruel twist of fate, after MacKay's loss to Jeb Bush, he unexpectedly became the Governor of Florida upon the untimely death of Lawton Chiles, serving during the transition period between the election in November and the inauguration in

January. As we mourned the passing of our revered Governor, we had to pick ourselves up and handle the day-to-day business of the state, while also handing the keys over to the guys who beat us. MacKay handled this with the utmost grace, carried on and turned this defeat into a victory, as always – leading by example.

Two years later, Florida's new constitutionally mandated term limits went into effect, meaning that more than half of the 120 seats in the Florida legislature would be "open" seats with no incumbent. After a few futile attempts to convince others to run for the open seat in my hometown, several suggested that I consider the job myself. Up to this point, I had always envisioned my lifelong role in politics as a staffer, even a political hack – what business did I have being a candidate? But as I thought about it, and talked to trusted friends and family, the possibility of transforming myself from aide to "principal" started to take hold. I knew that if I ever wanted to run for office, this was my chance, so I jumped off the cliff and never looked back.

* * *

Maybe characterizing my opponents as the "enemy" is too strong, but let's face it – by its very nature, politics drills down to two sides: Will you vote *for* me or *against* me? I had to come to grips with the realization that a certain percentage of people would vote *against* me, and despite my best efforts at separating politics from friendships, it was hard to stomach when I spied an opponents' sign in a friend's yard or recognized a neighbor's name on someone else's financial contribution list.

Clinging to the lessons I learned from my father and grandfather, I reminded myself that there are many reasons why people get involved in campaigns, and not all of those reasons are about opposing me. I was resolute in my refusal to enlist negative personal attacks *because I did not consider my opponents as enemies.* As it would turn out, this would be another very important lesson.

Dr. Todd Patterson, a respected neonatologist in Tallahassee, was one of my opponents in the Democratic primary for state House District 9. After the first primary, Dr. Patterson and I were the two candidates left standing. We then headed into a run-off to determine who would face the unopposed Republican, who had the luxury of building quite a war chest without a primary challenger. As the race tightened, my political advisers and financial supporters recommended a personal attack ad against Dr. Patterson. I distinctly recall many tense conversations, even arguments, as my campaign team advised me that we could not win the election without using negative, potentially damaging, information.

While I had been in politics long enough to know that negative campaign tactics work, I also remembered that important lesson from my dad's campaign – that victory can be found in defeat. As naïve as it may sound, I did not want to start my political career tearing someone's character apart. I had to look myself in the mirror each morning; and it was vastly more important to "win" by being true to myself...even if it meant possible defeat for my campaign.

After much wrangling, I stuck to my guns and refused to engage in personal attacks. Dr. Patterson and I battled on the airwaves and on the ground – our respective armies of friends and supporters feverishly knocking on doors, making phone calls, and waving signs at intersections around town. The election seemed close; but as returns started rolling in, early predictions appeared to be in our favor. While we waited nervously at our election night party for the election to be called, we were caught somewhat off-guard when Dr. Patterson showed up to congratulate me on my runoff victory. He also hand-delivered a campaign check in hopes of being the first to refill my coffers for the upcoming general election battle – only a month away.

Needless to say, I was touched by Dr. Patterson's personal

and financial support. His gesture sent a strong signal that a unified Democratic front would put our campaign in a strong position for the general election. One month later, I was honored to win and to have earned the opportunity to represent my hometown and Florida's capital city in the Florida House of Representatives.

* * *

But my relationship with Dr. Patterson did not end there. As the director of the neo-natal intensive care unit (NICU) at our local hospital, his chief responsibility involved overseeing the remarkable work of the doctors, nurses and therapists working every day to save the lives of our community's tiniest babies. After the election, he continued in this role, developing the NICU at Tallahassee Memorial Hospital into a highly respected regional leader in pre-term infant care.

Three years later, Dr. Patterson and I joined forces to battle an entirely different and much more important cause. Just as many women in business or politics, I waited almost too long to start a family. Shortly after my first re-election, my husband and I were overjoyed to learn that we were expecting our first child – with a due date in June, well after the close of the legislative session. Just a few months later, the skills of my former opponent were called into service when my water broke at the dangerous early gestational stage of 22 weeks. (The normal gestation for a full term infant is 38-42 weeks.)

Dr. Patterson appeared at our bedside to advise us of the dire implications and potential dangers of such an early-term birth. Though we delayed labor for only three days, Dr. Patterson's calming presence in the delivery room made the difference for us, as our child's life hung in the balance. We watched in awe as his steady and experienced hands inserted a breathing tube into our tiny baby, who only weighed 1 pound, 3.7 ounces. For the next four months, Dr. Patterson and his incredible team of doctors, nurses and therapists stood with us every step of the way, as we nursed and prayed our miracle baby to health.

My husband and I remain eternally grateful to Dr. Patterson, particularly as our "miracle baby" just celebrated his tenth birthday. Though our son has significant visual impairment; he is otherwise a happy, healthy and musically talented ten year-old. His precarious entry into this world gave me a very different perspective on life, but one that resonates with the foundation of my Presbyterian upbringing that "everything happens for a reason." Because of our previous relationship and the knowledge of his character, my husband and I did not hesitate in entrusting Dr. Patterson with our child's life.

Whether it's the political arena, the boardroom or simply everyday life, today's opponent or rival could very well end up as tomorrow's ally, partner, boss or, as in our case, a lifesaver.

* * *

The 2008 Democratic Primary in the U.S. presidential elections pitted U.S. Senator Hillary Clinton, the former First Lady and respected attorney, against the newcomer and one-term Senator from Illinois, Barack Obama. After a bitterly fought campaign – during which former President Bill Clinton slammed Obama's candidacy as a "fairy tale," while Obama sarcastically told Hillary Clinton that she was "likable enough" – the lines were drawn for the political fight that began to emerge during the Presidential primary. [58]

No matter which individual you supported as a Democrat, it was gut wrenching to watch, as the campaigns spared nothing in their battle to the top. When it became clear that Obama would win the nomination, the Clintons and the Obamas graciously put their acrimony aside for the good of the party and the nation as a whole. The two became a strong team as President and Secretary of State in the first Obama Administration.

The transformation of this relationship was illustrated

upon Clinton's retirement as Secretary of State at the conclusion of the President's first term. Obama called Clinton "a strong friend," and described their "great collaboration" over the last four years, saying, "I'm going to miss her." Clinton followed up by reporting that the two are "warm, close," with many shared experiences, including time in the White House. She later added, "any tensions are 'ancient history' because of ... the kind of people we all are, but also, we're professionals."[59]

Even in the highest office of the land, two former opponents provided a stellar example of setting aside past personal competition to focus on moving ahead.

* * *

While writing this chapter, I spent some time in Miami with my friend Chris Fulton, who owns and runs a very successful Florida based export company, supplying pipes, valves and fittings for the water industry in Latin America and the Caribbean. I have known Chris for over 20 years and watched him grow a one-man shop into an $8 million company employing 500 people, serving over 20 countries.

As we talked about our very divergent paths, I mentioned the work I was doing on this topic of opponents becoming allies, and he immediately made the analogy to the business world. Today's fierce business climate in the rapidly changing global economy often fosters similar rivalries to those found in the political arena. Any astute businessperson or successful salesman knows that today's competitor could very well turn out to be tomorrow's partner – and Chris has found this to be a very important point to remember: "My goal has been to establish a reputation for cooperating and winning, so that when the opportunity arises to score success working with a rival, the rival knows that we can be counted on," said Fulton. "When you deal with so many U.S. suppliers in so many small countries overseas, you stay friendly with everyone, including your rivals."

Whether you are an export business competing in a global

marketplace, or a small business trying to compete on Main Street, maintaining a friendly relationship while staying competitive and respectful could carry great potential far into the future. In the long run, building relationships that command respect will benefit both parties, whether it's during the competitive bid process or along the political spectrum.

The long race we call life is made easier for all when we view losing a big sale, important athletic game or a political battle as a vital lesson in the art of winning.

* * *

This lesson came full circle for me in 2010, when I re-entered the political arena after my "forced retirement" due to term limits. I decided to run for the Florida state Senate – in what turned out to be the very seat that my father had run for in 1974. After several successful fundraising quarters, everything changed when state and national Democratic leaders asked me to consider jumping into the statewide race for Chief Financial Officer.

What could have been a great opportunity in a normal year, turned out to be one of the hardest things I have ever done in my life: Democrat; down-ballot candidate; running against the 2010 national GOP wave – three strikes and you're out. I have no regrets – and know that the statewide campaign gave me important experience and exposure that is serving me well. While it is never easy to lose, I learned that all-important lesson that accepting defeat with grace *is* a victory.

I also learned not to bear a grudge against the loss, and instead use it as an ally of sorts. Rather than treating this political low-point as an enemy, it was my impetus to launch the next step in my journey. I now work with various organizations to provide political candidates in Southern states with the information and training I never had.[60] Just as I learned through Dr. Patterson that an opponent can become an ally, I have learned that victory comes in many forms – some of which initially look like a defeat.

(Many thanks to Serena Moyle for her inspiration and assistance in writing and in life. This would not have been possible without her.)

STEP ELEVEN:

Keep Your Head and Sense of Humor When All Around You Are Losing Theirs

By Carte Goodwin, former U.S. Senator from West Virginia

For those readers who have been carefully digesting Steps One through Ten that precede this chapter, you might have concluded that this book should be subtitled: *When Bad Things Happen to Good People*, or perhaps, *When Bad Things Happen to Imperfect Human Beings Who Mean Well.*

However, some times crisis can be borne of tremendous good news – a chance of a lifetime; or put another way, when the dog finally catches the car. As one of my political heroes, President John F. Kennedy, once noted, "The Chinese use two brush strokes to write the word 'crisis.' One brush stroke stands for danger; the other for opportunity."[61]

I'm living testament to that principle. A childhood dream almost literally was dumped in my lap. It was an extraordinary opportunity. But it came with considerable responsibilities and posed some serious challenges.

And I learned a powerful lesson for all forms of crisis management: **Keep your head and sense of humor when all around you are losing theirs**.

* * *

In July 2010, I was a 36-year-old attorney, recently returned to private practice after an incredible four-year stint as General Counsel to West Virginia Governor Joe Manchin. Then, West Virginians were saddened to learn of the passing of Senator Robert C. Byrd – one of the true lions of the Senate and West Virginia's most beloved public servant.

Governor Manchin had a strong interest in serving in the Senate (and ultimately, he would run for and win the seat); but as a man who believed in the sacred rites of our democracy, he did not want to appoint himself to the vacancy: He'd let the voters decide if they wanted to give him the honor of federal office.

But he also recognized that the people of West Virginia needed representation during the four months before a special election could be held. And much to my incredible honor, Governor Manchin appointed me to serve as West Virginia's junior U.S. Senator.

Senator Byrd cast quite a long shadow, and it was daunting to contemplate being appointed to fill the seat previously occupied by the longest serving legislative member in the history of the United States. I could not begin to replace Senator Byrd or ever hope to fill his enormous shoes, but what I could do was emulate his work ethic and commitment to West Virginia – which is precisely what I strove to do during my four months in Washington, a town ruled by Congress, Blackberries and Members-only elevators; and a place where fame (and infamy) can come and go in a matter of hours.

(Side note: Years before, former Oklahoma standout and Chicago Bulls forward Stacey King saw limited action in an NBA game, hitting a single free throw. That same night, his teammate

Michael Jordan poured in 69 points. Afterwards, King joked that he would always remember that game as the night that he and Jordan "combined for 70 points."[62] Similarly, rather that describing my term as "four months," I usually characterize it by saying that Senator Byrd and I combined to serve over 52 years in the United States Senate.)

Within days of my arrival, men and women I had studied in law school were introducing themselves to me, welcoming me as one of their own, then asking for my vote in the same sentence. And I wasn't alone; I was immediately put at the helm of a full Senate staff – many of whom had served for decades under Senator Byrd. I was given a personal secretary and press secretary – no longer would I be the one answering the phone in my own office. However, I declined the offer of a personal driver and walked myself to work.

In fact, as the august body's youngest member – and one who had never stood before the voters – I found it especially important to strongly resist all temptation to allow any of the unusual attention get to my head. Maintaining humility was critical, but also approaching the extraordinary opportunity with a healthy sense of humor would be a necessary prerequisite.

One area in which I applied these principles involved handling the unique challenges presented by the press. I had to adjust quickly to the media attention. I'd considered myself prepared for the press, after having spent four years as a senior staffer in the Governor's office, doing the occasional TV or radio interview. Yet, the appointment shot the level of attention into the stratosphere, with newspapers, television, blogs and everything in between weighing in with their thoughts on the relative merits of my appointment. Nothing was off-limits. To the delight of my buddies, one website offered an online poll debating where my looks stacked up against my fellow Senators, while a local West Virginia paper registered their enthusiasm for the appointment by describing it succinctly as "a letdown."

Indeed, the temporary burst of attention became so

intense that on the day that my appointment was announced, I briefly topped Google's "Hot Searches," besting former NBA star Penny Hardaway, the iPhone 4, and golfer "John Daly's pants." I haven't had the inclination to go back and find out why Daly's pants made the top ten that day.

After calling my brother in Illinois and asking him to drive home for the announcement two days later, he had to get time off from his new banking job, which he had just started earlier that week. The bank CEO was a little skeptical at my brother's justification for the leave request, at least until he turned on CNN that Friday.

Speaking of CNN, once your photograph and video is splashed across network and cable news, the suggestion that your wife had been making for years that you should quit cutting your own hair finally begins to sink in. In hindsight, a pair of those Daly pants might have distracted viewers from the hatchet job that my old clippers had done the previous week.

By the time I arrived in D.C., the Senate was embroiled in a contentious debate regarding the extension of federal unemployment assistance for millions of Americans. Following weeks of deliberation and the inability to break a Republican filibuster, the measure was scheduled to come to the floor for a vote immediately following my swearing in ceremony on July 21. 57 members of my party's caucus were supporting the bill, along with two members of the minority party; given this mathematical breakdown, it was characterized by the media that I would be casting the "deciding" vote.

With nearly 20,000 West Virginians in dire need of this temporary assistance, along with over two million Americans, I was inclined to support the extension, an inclination that was bolstered by my subsequent research and review of the legislative materials. As such, I was expected to be the final vote necessary to end debate on the bill and pass the measure. Accordingly, the realization dawned on me that I was playing a role of outsized importance on this, my first vote as a member of the Senate.

And as I strode onto the floor of the Senate to take my oath, it was easy to become overwhelmed by the moment – the sight of my wife Rochelle and my entire family beaming in the gallery, emotional thoughts on the sudden passing of my father just three months earlier, the gravity of the situation itself, and my role in it all coming together in a very serious way. Yet, as the roll call began, all of my confidence and preparation soon gave way to a more pressing concern:

How do I vote?

About a half-mile from where I grew up in Mt. Alto, West Virginia, there was an auction house that was packed to the rafters every Friday and Saturday night. As anyone who has attended an auction there will tell you, the most important rule you need to know is *how* to bid – and of course, how *not* to bid. In many auctions, a raised arm may work for newcomers, while a familiar nod would suffice for the regulars. Similarly, depending upon the auction, the scratch of an ear, raising a thumb, or taking off a jacket could successfully submit a bid (or unsuccessfully, if done unknowingly). The best way to learn these subtle differences is to watch.

Indeed, that is precisely what I had planned to do (to the extent that the mechanical process of voting had even dawned on me at that point). And yet, as the clerk continued calling the roll, it quickly became apparent that there was no discernable system for casting your vote. Moreover, there did not seem to be any particular order to the names being called out by the clerk. Instead, my fellow Senators would crowd in front of the clerk's desk and offer various hand signals, nods, and head shakes that apparently only the clerk could decipher. Others simply strolled by quickly offering the same. There was at least one thumbs-up accompanied by the word "No," and I could have sworn I saw someone give the old Bobby Cox steal signal.

I suppose I had anticipated a mechanical system like the

one that I had grown accustomed to working with the West Virginia legislature during my time in the Governor's office. The benefits of such a system were evident – you hit a button (which was color coded to guide you), got immediate feedback on an illuminated board displaying your vote, along with helpfully displaying the votes of your colleagues.

No such luck.

So here I was, having received coverage on everything from *NBC Nightly News* to *Vanity Fair*, filling the seat of a certifiable legend in the world's greatest deliberative body, and having the important responsibility of breaking a filibuster (all of which led Google users to deem me more interesting than John Daly's pants), and yet no one had thought to tell me *how* to vote. Fearful of having any signal misinterpreted, I walked to the clerk and carefully offered my "aye" vote, which, when reported aloud by the clerk, prompted the clan of rowdy West Virginians amassed in the gallery to break into cheers (prompting, in turn, calls for order from the chair and stern looks from the Sergeant at Arms).

Today, a framed copy of that very roll call hangs outside my office, a reminder not only of my small role in helping to pass this important legislation, but also of the first rule in any auction house – knowing how to bid.

* * *

I garnered many more memories during the remainder of my time in the Senate, some personal (like the birth of my beautiful daughter), others professional (such as the privilege, as a practicing lawyer, of standing on the floor of the Senate chamber and casting an "aye" for the confirmation of a Supreme Court Justice). It was, and it will always remain, my enduring privilege to have represented West Virginia in that esteemed body.

I know that there will always be a strong pull to feel, as I did when I cast that deciding vote on extending unemployment benefits, that I would be making a difference in the lives of West Virginians – the people I know, that I grew up with, that are my neighbors, many of whom have seen hard times while our economy struggled. After November, when my term was over and I was back in West Virginia, some of these folks would approach me, look me in the eye and say "thanks," telling me how I had made a difference in their lives. I realized that was something that I will always strive to do, even without the title of "Senator" in front of my name.

My brief foray onto politics' biggest stage also taught me a valuable lesson about the dignity of all individuals. Whether you are a hardworking person struggling to keep his head above water during an unprecedented economic crisis, or a new U.S. Senator struggling to figure out how to cast a vote properly, we are all equal in the eyes of God. That's why, especially during times of crisis, it is so critical to take your job seriously, but not yourself too seriously. A dollop of humor with a strong dose of humility is the perfect recipe for surviving the crisis/opportunity of a lifetime.

* * *

Humor and humility are not simply reserved for bucket list experiences such as my own. They can come particularly in handy during harrowing crises such as described by this book's co-authors. And they have been used successfully by some of the nation's most prominent public figures.

No modern politician has been more effective in using humor to deflect controversy and survive crisis than the President of my childhood, Ronald Reagan. While his prior career in Hollywood trained him to apply wit in sensitive situations (or when dealing with a chimpanzee named Bonzo), it was an extraordinary personal crisis that demonstrated the power of his wisecracking charm to a concerned nation.

In March 1981, just a few weeks into his first term in office, an assassination attempt was made on the President's life.

A stray bullet struck Reagan, who suffered a punctured lung and heavy internal bleeding. With the 24/7 news media in its infancy – CNN had just been launched in the prior year – the eyes of all Americans were focused on their television sets, awaiting updates on the President's condition. While doctors struggled to save his life, Reagan offered some clever jokes to assure the nation he would be OK.

As he was wheeled into the operating room, Reagan looked up at doctors and nurses at George Washington University Hospital and quipped, "I hope you're all Republicans." After surviving the assassination attempt, he told his wife Nancy, "Honey, I forgot to duck."[63] Reagan's poise under fire – literally – resulted in surging approval ratings; empowering him to pass his ambitious, yet controversial, economic agenda.[64]

Reagan's sense of humor also served him well in a much different kind of crisis – an existential threat to his political viability. During his first presidential debate in his 1984 re-election bid against former Vice President Walter Mondale, Reagan appeared tired and listless. Questions were raised subsequently about his capacity to continue to hold office, particularly how his advanced age was affecting his ability to serve in the world's most powerful position. His large lead in the polls over Mondale shrank to an uncomfortable single-digit margin.[65]

As the second presidential debate commenced, all eyes were on Reagan to see if he could rebound. And then the highly anticipated question was asked of the President: whether his age would affect his leadership abilities during a major crisis. Reagan's response? "Not at all...and I want you to know that also I will not make age an issue in this campaign. I am not going to exploit, for political purposes, my opponent's youth and inexperience." The one-liner diffused the crisis; and after the debate, Mondale never threatened the President's lead again. Reagan won every state in the nation, with the exception of Mondale's home of Minnesota.[66]

Humor also has empowered some in the public eye to escape the grasp of withering scandal. Former Louisiana Governor Edwin Edwards practically built his public career on it, appealing to many people as a lovable rogue who spent the bulk of his four terms as Governor fending off dozens of political challenges and corruption charges with his characteristic dry wit (much of which may not be suitable for print).

Once describing a political opponent as "so slow it takes him an hour and a half to watch *60 Minutes*," when Edwards beat former Klansman David Duke in a famous campaign, Edwards' supporters sported bumper stickers reading, "Vote for the Crook: It's Important." Later, during (one of) his trials on federal corruption charges, Edwards arrived at the courthouse in a mule drawn carriage, remarking that it was symbolic of the speed and intellect of the federal judicial system. When asked at yet another trial to comment on the judicial proceedings, Edwards said, "I never speak ill of dead people or live judges." These sorts of outlandish statements and Edwards' outsized personality certainly should not serve as a model for public service or crisis management. Yet, in its own unique way, his particular brand of humor revealed a sincerity and lack of pretense that apparently resonated with voters for decades.

Equally evident in Edwards' tale, however, is the more important lesson here: Humor is no substitute for sound judgment and honest dealing, a lesson that Governor Edwards learned firsthand when he was convicted of various federal charges in the 1990s. I wouldn't recommend anyone accused of a horrible crime to joke even lightly, nor should anyone employ humor immediately following moments of natural calamity or national tragedy. Additionally, due to the nature of the 24/7 media – rushing to publish stories with sensational impact – leaders must to be careful not to tell jokes that can be taken out of context and allow adversaries to score political points.

This phenomenon is particularly true when a public figure makes a joke that plays into the perceived flaws about that individual. Take Ronald Reagan, for example. Even the Great

Communicator could slip up, as he did in 1984 when he was caught during a microphone check for his Saturday radio address making a joke about bombing the Soviet Union: "My fellow Americans, I am pleased to tell you today that I've signed legislation that will outlaw Russia forever. We begin bombing in five minutes." Continual replay of the tape exacerbated Reagan's reputation as too belligerent, too eager to provoke a nuclear holocaust.[67]

More recently, renowned actress and humanitarian, Ashley Judd – who was considering, but later abandoned, a bid for the U.S. Senate in Kentucky against Minority Leader Mitch McConnell – was caught joking about how she and her Scottish husband "winter in Scotland...We are smart like that." Anyone listening understood the irony – who would want to spend winter in the cold, frozen Scottish climate? But political operatives effectively took the joke out of context to reinforce their depiction of a Hollywood elitist out of touch with real Kentuckians.[68]

* * *

But while I recommend that humor be used only in appropriate situations, let's not take even that admonition too seriously. At a time when Americans are fed up with politics – when Congressional approval is at all-time lows, below that of Brussels sprouts, and just barely above root canals;[69] we all could enjoy a little more *intentional* humor mixed in with our policy discussions.

Most of all, maintaining a sense of humor, as well as a little humility, can be an invaluable tonic when dealing with a difficult crisis. My co-authors have explained how even what may appear to be the worst personal calamity can often be a tremendous learning experience. I can attest that the opportunity of a lifetime will only be enjoyable if you don't allow good fortune to change your outlook on life and your understanding of others. The best way to avoid any negative effects is to always remind yourself of your core values, stick to them, and take all of your experiences – good and bad – with a healthy grain of salt.

And always understand that a good laugh – whether shared with others or chuckled silently – can be a powerful tool to transcending a tense situation, strengthening personal bonds, and most of all, keeping yourself sane, while the world spins in its glorious insanity.

STEP TWELVE:

Spread Good Will to Prevent the Next Crisis

By Jennifer Mann, former Pennsylvania State Representative

In the midst of my tenure in office as a Pennsylvania state representative, a statewide scandal uprooted the political landscape like a tornado of Wizard of Oz proportions. For those of us unscathed and continuing work in Pennsylvania's Capitol, we were still left with a "we're-not-in-Kansas-anymore" reality that proved tense, to say the least.

"Bonusgate" was the pithy pet name for a massive investigation into political corruption in which millions of taxpayer dollars were misappropriated as bonuses to legislative staffers who were campaigning while on the clock.

The investigation wound together deceit, cover-ups and political finger pointing into a whirlwind that swept up some of the state's longest serving lawmakers. Some of my colleagues caught up in the storm of rapid-fire reporter questions and constituent scorn landed not in Oz, but in jail. Many more were thrown out of office, as voters took their anger to the polls and elected one of the largest freshmen classes in the state's history. It was a scary time to be a state representative.

Just as a point of reference, I should note that Pennsylvania is one of the few states to employ a full-time legislature and no term limits. For those who choose to run for office and succeed, there is a scary realization that your career and income is suddenly in the hands of voters. And while I will defend the importance of maintaining a full-time legislature, I'll admit that the overlying threat of getting the potential "pink slip" at the polls leads to a protective instinct that's palpable around the Capitol. The desire to survive creates a sub-culture of risk-taking, and even forces a select few to cross the line between right and wrong. This is my assessment of what creates corruption, at least in this case.

When the Attorney General released the first of many findings in the Bonusgate investigation, careers and reputations were ruined almost instantly, and the career carnage kept coming. Fortunately, I was a Bonusgate bystander, a safe distance from the action.

Until one morning, I wasn't.

When the reporter contacted me to get my side of the story on the juicy tidbit of information he had, supposedly tying my top aide to Bonusgate, I responded openly and with the same nothing-to-hide style that was the core of my political reputation.

Still, by the time I hung up the phone, my stomach was in my throat. The mere thought of the article hitting newsstands consumed my thoughts and nerves. I tried to hope for the best, like a sidebar blurb buried somewhere in the back of the paper.

The resulting banner headline that greeted me soon after was the antithesis of any style or reputation I had cultivated, and it was far from hidden. Instead, it alluded to a direct link between my senior staffer and some of those who had fallen the farthest in our state's scandal.

In reality, the full-color, front-page exposé was all style, no substance. The emails cited were taken out of context. The source faced criminal conviction and had already established a jailhouse-snitch notoriety for trying to invite company into his misery. And the fact was that my staffer had not pocketed any tax dollars for his time spent on the campaign trail.

Still, the timing of the story and the wording in the headline alone suggested a cover up that could only serve to outrage vexed voters even more.

I processed the article like a boxing match transpiring in slow motion. I saw the heavyweight square up, cock his arm and start to pivot slowly as his fist came straight for my face. The best I could hope for was a permanent black eye, but I'd seen this fight before, and it typically ended in a total knockout.

My phone rang before impact. It was my staffer and subject of aforementioned article. We had a conversation that I vaguely recall as, "Oh crap! Oh crap! Oh crap!"

We arrived at our typically upbeat office to find it shrouded in silent, wide-eyed worry. The atmosphere quickly became akin to a funeral parlor, with me thrust unwittingly into the role of mourning widow. Friends and colleagues stopped by, offering carefully worded encouragement and quietly gauging my reaction.

The uncertainty of perception hung like a haze. Then the clouds formed into a brainstorm, and I was showered with advice from those who felt protective and invested.

Looking back, the deluge of suggestions was a nice reminder of my incredible support system. Everyone who offered a solution was qualified to do so. The points of view were valuable, and the concern sincere. Many encouraged me to make my response as public as the newspaper article by sending out a press release or scheduling a news conference.

The haze eventually lifted, and the approach became clear. I had years of availability and honesty to draw on. If there was ever a time to tap into my reserve of good karma, this was it.

I ducked to avoid the punch and came out of my corner ready to fight the only way I knew how: one-on-one and with a direct approach.

My staff and I had a full schedule that day, and I intended to keep it and add to it if possible. My reputation was not one of controlled environments and scheduled press availability. Now was not the time to become sheltered and protected.

Still, marching out and into my first event of the day was like that first frigid step into a cold swimming pool. Doing my best to mask my uncertainty and hyper-awareness, I felt pleasantly surprised when the first greetings I received were warm, friendly and even a little protective. As the day wore on, the reception I received from my constituents bolstered my confidence. I started to realize that while I was focused on the potential damage to my future, the people I encountered that day seemed more focused on my past. Meeting people face-to-face and hearing their encouragement and support made it clear that reputations are not nearly as disposable as today's headlines.

The crisis – that at one point seemed devastating – had no real legs. I pounded the pavement and met my potential detractors head on, while the headline, I can only imagine, lined a birdcage or something of the sort.

This example, of course, was not my only crisis during my 13 years in office.

However, I am proud to say it was one of the worst. By constantly investing in my relationships and reputation, I found it increasingly easier to weather any storms that came my way.

When I retired from office, I told my successor that one of the best things that can happen to a newly elected official is to have a great example to follow. A tongue-in-cheek snippet of advice? Sure. For me, having a strong predecessor really did set the standard for my own reputation management early on.

Elected to office in my 20s, I took over for Charlie Dent, a well-liked Republican in a primarily Democratic district. Congressman Dent, as he's known at the time of this writing, is the kind of guy who still returns phone calls. He's still regularly spotted throughout the district; and while his constituency has grown, I believe his accessibility remains the same.

I knew that if I followed Charlie's example, I would have success. I don't think I knew at the time that good-old fashioned listening and respect for others would end up as my greatest defense against crisis in my career.

I was also blessed with an instinct to protect my reputation and relationships very early on. This made it easy for me to keep those things a priority as my public position chipped away at my privacy. If you were lacking that instinct, I'd still recommend putting your character and the many characters that come into your life high on your priority list. It's not easy; maintenance of both is best performed on a person-to-person basis. When I meet people, no matter how quick the encounter, I want them to walk away feeling something good about me, but also about themselves.

To really benefit from your karma reserves, you must understand that true good will shouldn't come with an ulterior motive. In fact, I would wager a guess that if you lack authenticity in your approach, it would not be as successful. Especially as our world moves farther into the virtual realm, there's no substitute for genuine good will and face time.

Former President Bill Clinton is a good example of the power of being a true "people person." After the Clinton administration ended, Dan Emmet, a member of the President's security detail, described the unprecedented security concerns when Clinton insisting on jogging in unsecured areas. He also made note of the real reason for the presidential detours: "His running was for meeting the public as much as it was for exercise," Emmet recalled.[70]

Ironically, Clinton's penchant for the public may have led

to his most notorious crisis: As Former British Prime Minister Tony Blair wrote in his memoir, the 42nd President had an "inordinate interest in and curiosity about people."[71]

Still, even after Clinton's curiosity for Monica Lewinsky became the focal point of his presidency, the public was forgiving. In fact, Gallup recorded the highest approval ratings of the Clinton Administration right smack dab in the middle of the Lewinsky scandal and subsequent impeachment proceedings.[72]

During that time, Clinton chose not to hide. Shortly after the scandal broke, he took to the podium and delivered a determined State of the Union Address. With Congressional support waning, he moved his focus to foreign policy, an arena that allowed him more unilateral control. Despite ongoing impeachment hearings, the President stayed politically active, and in turn, publicly appealing.

Whether Clinton's charisma was the true Teflon that kept crisis from sticking to his reputation is debatable, but most agree it didn't hurt. Clinton's proactive approach with the public certainly seemed to pay off and has become part of his legacy.

Applying good will should start the day you take on your leadership role. Or, if you were already prudent enough to be refining your reputation from the start, your investment should increase exponentially with your responsibility.

Proactively get involved with whomever you serve. Isn't it wonderful when you meet someone you admire, and he or she turns out to be a nice person? Be that nice person.

One of the most selfless acts you can do for others is to truly listen to what they have to say, without letting your own response interfere. Once you have an understanding of what's important to your audience, then you can serve them more effectively, and in turn, build trust. Once you've earned the trust of those you serve and built a reputation of authenticity, you position yourself as a leader who puts others' needs before your own ambitions.

Socrates said, "Rule worthy of might." Later, Marvel Comics applied the same theme to Spiderman with the widely quoted phrase, "With great power comes great responsibility." Someone should preface these quotes with something along the lines of, "the more power you get, the more out of touch you can become." It's an easy trap to fall into and has provided the premise for more than one hit reality TV show.

In true reality, as you advance in a leadership role, it is almost shocking how quickly you can become removed from the "real world." Sometimes an increased amount of tasks stand between you and the ability to connect with people. Sometimes, more people stand between you and your constituents, clients or customers. Investing in your relationships and reputation takes conscious and applied effort and a genuine desire to connect with others.

Much like a MasterCard commercial, spending time to solidify relationships may come with a cost early on, but drawing on that support and reputational capital in a time of crisis is truly priceless.

AFTERWORD

By Jason Grill, former Missouri State Representative

In the preceding chapters, the themes of loss and redemption run through the text as an omnipresent thread. Whether you've suffered an existential blow or a temporal setback; whether you've been exposed in an embarrassingly public way, or hurt in a private, interpersonal matter; adversity can be personally devastating, and the desire for rehabilitation or even atonement can take on acute urgency.

One of my own biggest setbacks in life is one that has been shared by nearly every other individual in the political arena, and certainly by most in any other field of work or play in which competition is involved.

I lost.

Indeed, while most media consumers tend to buy into the myth that politics is just like sports – wins and losses are to be shaken off immediately, as we get back on our feet for the next race – the truth is that losing hurts. I lost a job that I really loved, in which I felt I was making a real difference.

* * *

I had entered the political world at the age of 25, just one year older than the minimum required by the State of Missouri to serve in its state House of Representatives. Political blood didn't run in the family; and the only involvement I had in the arena as an adolescent was putting up the occasional yard sign in the front yard, voting in the *Weekly Reader* election poll in grade school and serving as Vice President of my high school's student government.

But after a stint in the Clinton White House, politics was in my blood. In 2004, I was recruited to run for the Missouri House of Representatives, I took the name on the ballot plunge and jumped in the deep end of the pool.

I lost my first race against a popular three-term incumbent Republican in a deeply GOP legislative district by only 224 votes out of nearly 20,000 cast: a 50 to 49% final outcome. This was the closest race for a seat in the Missouri House of Representatives in the entire election cycle.

Within a few weeks, I signed back up to run for the same seat; and two years later – with the incumbent term-limited – I captured the hotly contested open seat by a 20-point margin. In 2008, I ran for reelection unopposed, the best kind of campaign for any politician.

My four years of service in the Missouri House of Representatives was an extraordinary experience. I served on prestigious committees, worked with colleagues on both sides of the aisle, and reveled in the opportunities for constituent service. My greatest moment in government came during my second term, when the Governor signed legislation I had sponsored that expanded access to life-changing autism diagnoses, treatment and therapy. I had an opportunity to make a difference, and I took it. I felt like a very lucky man.

But luck can run both ways.

The political pendulum in America shifted directions dramatically in 2010. At the height of the Tea Party revolution, President Barack Obama was polling only at a 42% favorable rating in my legislative district, with an even lower 37% job approval. Meanwhile, Republican registrants outnumbered Democrats by a margin of 49 to 39%. While my pollster assured me that due to my high name recognition and approval ratings, I was the safest state legislative incumbent they worked for in 2010; she also warned me that a very effective negative attack would be to tie me to the "liberal" Obama agenda.

And it worked. Mailer after mailer, commercial after commercial, linked me to the President and his "radical" agenda. You would have thought we were best friends and eating dinner together every night. Ultimately, out of the 15,000 votes cast in my district, I lost by 174. The exact same 50 to 49% outcome as my first race.

Needless to say, I was in shock. The moments after losing, I couldn't stop thinking about all the things I could have done better. Had I made just a few different decisions, I could have squeaked out my own narrow victory: Why didn't I mail handwritten postcards to all the individuals I met, as I did in the 2006 race? Why didn't I personally knock on more doors, as I did in 2006? Why did I let favorable poll results and what others were saying about my lead during the homestretch affect my focus and campaign work ethic?

I was at a crossroads. How should I handle this unexpected blow?

As a baseball nut, I couldn't get out of my mind two highly publicized incidents involving my home state's Hall of Fame heroes, Stan Musial and George Brett. Each man provided the opposite archetype for handling adversity.

George Brett, my favorite baseball player of all time, had the more famous – some might say *infamous* – incident. On July 24th, 1983, the Kansas City Royals third baseman stepped up to the plate in the top of the ninth inning with two out, trailing the New York Yankees 4 to 3 at Yankee Stadium. Brett, a left-handed hitter, crouched down deep into his much-mimicked batting stance and blasted a dramatic home run off Yankees' closer Goose Gossage to give the Royals a 5-4 lead.

As Brett rounded the bases, Billy Martin, the charismatic and often erratic manager of the Yankees, looked over to one of his coaches and winked. He had been waiting for this moment: He knew that Brett had been applying too much pine tar on his bat, in violation of a little known league rule. Martin appealed to home plate umpire Tim McClelland, and the ump agreed, calmly signaling Brett out. The home run was nullified; the game was over; and the Yankees were victorious.

Decades before the advent of YouTube, the video of Brett's reaction became a staple of sports television. Brett sprinted out of the dugout to argue with McClelland with a fire in his eyes at the level of a ten-story blaze. His fury became etched in baseball lore forever.[73]

Stan Musial's moment occurred nearly three decades earlier, in 1954. The legendary St. Louis Cardinals slugger was at the plate late in the game, as his squad trailed their archrival Chicago Cubs 3 to 0 at Wrigley Field. Musial appeared to have hit a line drive double down the right field line scoring Wally Moon from second base. Moments later, however, the first base umpire, Lee Ballanfant, called the ball foul. Even the biased home crowd knew the call was wrong. Chaos erupted as several Cardinals charged out of the dugout, and the team's shortstop and manager were thrown out of the game.[74]

Musial meanwhile calmly walked over to the umpire crew chief to inquire about the ruling. He assured the ump that an honest mistake was made, and it wasn't anyone's fault. After play resumed, Musial returned to the plate and hit another rope to nearly the same exact place in right field. This time, the umpire called the ball fair; and as karma would have it, the Cards went on to win the game.[75]

When the "pine tar" game was replayed after an appeal to league officials, George Brett couldn't return because he'd been ejected for his actions. Because Stan Musial kept his cool, he was allowed to return to the plate, and help his team win the ballgame.

* * *

After my 2010 election loss, every fiber in my mind and body wanted to react along the lines of my childhood hero. I too wanted to charge after my adversaries. I too wanted to attack and blame other people. In some ways, I too, like Brett, felt cheated.

But fortunately, I knew down deep that Stan the Man had the correct plan. I kept my head down, maintained my cool and moved on. I knew that some times close calls would go my way, and other times they wouldn't. Like Musial, I chose to stay in the game.

As my fellow co-authors have discussed over the previous chapters, success in politics – or in any vocation for that matter – often revolves around how we perform during our worst times of crisis, when we face the most difficult forms of adversity. They have offered the reader a number of insightful lessons from their own experiences; on specific ways they have transcended crisis and scandal to build greater opportunities for their future. Some have even suggested that the most awful moments of their lives provided some of the most invaluable lessons for their futures.

So I offer you this closing thought: If you find yourself in a time of adversity – or indeed, if you are currently struggling through crisis now – remember the example of Stan Musial. Those who maintain their grace, their honor, and their respect for others, even while the world appears to be conspiring against them, are usually the ones who can survive even the worst crises.

The Recovering Politician's Twelve-Step Program for Surviving Crisis

A SUMMARY

Step One: *Hold Your Breath...With Your Mouth Shut*: Before you plunge into rapid response, make a careful assessment of the situation, asking whether this particular episode will blow over, and whether any additional oxygen you provide it could only fuel the fire of crisis or scandal.

Step Two: *Tell the Truth: Don't Even Go Near the Line*: Lies, spin, truth shading, and exaggeration are accepted components of today's political and media dialogue. But as a crisis first develops, it is critical to be completely honest in order to keep from empowering your rivals, the press, or – worst of all – law enforcement to use a false statement against you, transforming a small crisis into a much bigger scandal.

Step Three: *Lean Into, and Learn from, Your Crisis*: While imminent disclosure of an embarrassing circumstance might first seem to be a devastating blow to your career or reputation; more often than not, the crisis is the beginning of your journey, not the end. Learn from your mistakes and embrace them to transcend your circumstances. Your "worst day" indeed might lead to unexpected triumph.

Step Four: *Make an Emotional Connection*: Simple recitation of facts and figures often will not be sufficient to transcend a crisis.

Whether it is a highly publicized scandal, or an intimate family dispute, identifying and sharing an emotional connection is critical to winning support and establishing credibility. As you craft your message, remember to focus on the heart, as well as the mind.

Step Five: *Be First to Frame your Narrative in Your Own Voice, with Facts and Sincerity*: The best defense often means going on offense. Jump out early and "break" the story before your opponents or competition have a chance. Since storytelling is the most powerful form of communication and persuasion, controlling the narrative of your scandal is a critical element of successful crisis management.

Step Six: *Develop a Clear, Concise Message, and Stick To It*: Once you have developed your response to a crisis, it is essential that you not waver from your developed message. Repeating the same talking points may frustrate your interviewer or even bore you to tears, but veering from that message can often open up new battles that you don't want to fight.

Step Seven: *Own Your Mistakes, Take Responsibility and Sincerely Say "I'm Sorry"*: Nothing is more powerful in a major public crisis, or any small interpersonal dispute, than the acceptance of responsibility and a statement of sincere contrition. This is the first necessary step towards rehabilitation.

Step Eight: *Present Your Fix-it Plan*: Saying sorry isn't always sufficient; it is often necessary to publicly outline a plan of action for remediating a crisis, ensuring skeptical stakeholders that the mistake at issue will never happen again. Developing a clear, concise, and credible fix-it plan can be essential to moving past any scandal.

Step Nine: *Listen to the People You Trust And Ignore All Others*: In approaching crisis management, you'll be bombarded with offers of advice, much of it not serving your interests. Listen carefully to the people you trust, and hire a professional if practical; but ignore the noise from others.

<u>Step Ten</u>: *Don't Bear Grudges; Yesterday's Enemy Can Be Tomorrow's Ally*: Perhaps the most difficult thing for anyone to do in order to transcend a scandal is to forgive those that hurt you, and even more importantly, yourself. Bearing grudges, plotting revenge, and/or seeking your own retributive pound of flesh are historical recipes for personal unhappiness and exacerbating the existing crisis. And you never know: a former rival or critic might one day become a valued friend.

<u>Step Eleven</u>: *Keep Your Head and Sense of Humor When All Around You Are Losing Theirs*: While a crisis might seem personally overwhelming, it is critical to keep your cool and a strong dose of humility. In many cases, a sense of humor, particularly of the self-deprecating variety, can be both your best offense and defense. As you soberly address the ramifications of the crisis, remember to never take yourself too seriously.

<u>Step Twelve</u>: *Spread Good Will to Prevent the Next Crisis*: Understand that while your current crisis might be unprecedented, it will very likely not be your last. Learn the lessons of the mistakes you've made in the past and proactively spread good will to help insulate yourself or your organization from the next potential crisis.

Twelve Step Program for Meditation Through Crisis

By Lisa Miller, Mind/Body Health Educator

As a professional and mother dedicated to helping people emotionally navigate through everyday crises, I used to ask myself how I could become part of a world of solutions that create peace, if my internal emotional world felt turbulent. How could I have happy, peaceful relationships if my own happiness and equanimity were dependent on external factors that were fleeting at best: sugary foods, new jobs, new diets, vacations, new anything? How could I represent health and vitality without *living it*?

Among the many resources I've discovered, it turns out that effective solutions for a chaotic inner landscape can begin with unbelievably simple strategies. One is called breathing. Who knew? Another is silence. My experience is not only that these practices are magical remedies for daily stress reduction and crisis management; they also can serve as a foundation for how we extend ourselves forward into our personal and professional relationships, into the community, into the world. How we lay the groundwork to walk with balance through chaos and change.

Breathe and be quiet, repeat. There is no club to join, no equipment to buy, no complicated process to learn; it involves just sitting quietly every day and allowing yourself to clear your mind, and in effect, to rewire your primitive fight/flight response, to strengthen your heart, immune system, and spiritual life. Practiced for thousands of years, meditation and deep breathing are not about forcing the mind to be quiet; they're about finding the silence and peace already there and letting them lead the way through daily life.

Here are brief instructions for a personal meditation and deep breathing practice to help you respond, rather than react, to your environment, tap into your deep inner wisdom, manage crisis, and build a happier life:

Step One: Pick a location where you know you won't be disturbed for 20-30 minutes. Set a gentle sounding alarm to let you know when the 20-30 minutes have expired. I use the xylophone or crickets feature on my phone.

Step Two: Sit comfortably and close your eyes.

Step Three: Silently ask yourself each of the following questions twice:

- Who am I?

- What do I want? (The answers might be material, physical, emotional, ethereal…anything you would like to see fulfilled.)

- What is my purpose in this life?

- How can I help? How can I serve?

(There is no need to "think" of answers. Some may come; some may not. Asking the questions is the essential part of this practice so that the deeper answers can come eventually. Often our decisions don't come from a deep place of knowing, but rather from the less reliable ego place; this practice of repeatedly asking and waiting to see what comes brings the wisdom of your heart and soul into your awareness.)

<u>Step Four</u>: Now let go of the questions and answers and let the universe work out the details.

<u>Step Five</u>: Take 10 Slooooooooow Deeeeeep Breaths:

- <u>Inhale</u>: To do this, sloooooowly fill your belly with oxygen extending it forward as if it's a balloon you are inflating. Fully inflated, you can take in no more air – you are completely full. Hold this for 3 seconds.

- <u>Exhale:</u> To do this, release your air slooooooowly. It's harder to exhale slowly than to inhale slowly, but you control your breath, not the other way around. At the end of your exhale, push the remaining air out of your belly by using your belly muscles to push your belly button down toward your seat and behind you to your spine.

- Hold this emptiness for 3 seconds; like the space between musical notes, there is silence and stillness here, but it's alive and about to lead to the next inspired movement.

- Now your next breath comes spontaneously from this place of pause. Repeat; this new breath feels really good.

<u>Step Six</u>: Breathe normally now and sit in the stillness and fullness you created with your breath, and merely focus on the relaxed breath entering your nostrils and the breath leaving your body. With each inhale, bring your awareness to the vibration of your inhale that sounds like "So", and the exhale that sounds like "Hum". *Listen* for this vibration rather than *focus* on it. Let yourself be breathed.

<u>Step Seven</u>: Listen for these "So" and "Hum" vibrations or "sounds" as you inhale and exhale. This will allow you to let go of your mind chatter and to focus on your stillness.

175

Step Eight: If your mind wanders (and it will for the first three weeks!), just gently bring your focus back to your breath and to the "So" and "Hum" vibrations it's creating.

Step Nine: By sitting in silence and really breathing for just 20-30 minutes out of 24 hours in the day, scientific evidence shows compellingly the effects of decreased fight/flight response through lowered blood pressure, reduced anxiety, and diminished production of the stress hormone cortisol.

Step Ten: It's worth a try for at least 21 days in a row. If you don't like it after 21 days, re-evaluate; however, I think you'll be convincing your family and friends to try it by that point. Come on: All the cool kids are doing it!

Step Eleven: For more about integrating mind-heart health, use the following inspiring and informative resources: *Secrets of Meditation* by David Ji, *Chakra Healing* by Rosalyn Bruyere, *Free to Love Free to Heal*, by Dr. David Simon, M.D, *Perfect Health*, by Dr. Deepak Chopra, M.D, and *Seat of the Soul*, by Gary Zukav.

Step Twelve: Come to a workshop. You can find a great one at my Web site.[76]

Twelve Step Program to Survive a Financial Crisis

By David B. Snyder, CLU, JD, Financial Adviser at Northwestern Mutual

BASICS

Step One: *Save Cash.* Ensure you have the cash reserves necessary to survive a financial crisis. You should have three to six months worth of expenses saved in cash specifically for this purpose. Begin NOW to build up cash reserves.

Step Two: *Pay off Debts.* Carrying debt will only exacerbate a financial crisis because cash flow will likely be quite tight. Make sure you are addressing your debt situation within the bounds of your current cash flow and taking positive steps each month to rid yourself of that debt.

A CRISIS OF THE WORST KIND: Losing a job due to accident, sickness or injury; a death prior to life expectancy; or the need for chronic nursing care.

Step Three: Make sure you have enough *Long Term Disability Coverage.* This type of insurance will provide you income during a disability that is due to accident, sickness or injury. In most cases, the coverage provided by an employer is not enough, and is considered taxable income. There is a great need to supplement and maximize your income in the event of a disability.

Step Four: Make sure you have enough *Life Insurance Coverage.*

Nothing can prepare you for this type of crisis, but having the right amount of coverage will provide you the options to work through this situation. Be guided by the following principle: For every $1,000/month you want to provide to a surviving spouse, or other beneficiary, you need $250,000 of life insurance coverage. Thus, to provide a surviving spouse with $6,000/month, you should be carrying $1,500,000 of coverage.

Step Five: To protect your long-term savings, make sure you have *Long Term Care Coverage*. If the need for chronic nursing care hits your family, the best way to survive is to have proper long term care insurance coverage. Without it, expect the cost of care to be (in today's dollars) $75,000/year. That will very quickly eat away at other savings, and without such coverage, the crisis will snowball.

GROWING YOUR ASSETS: It's hard to survive a crisis without proper money management. And the more you save today, the more a crisis can be eased.

Step Six: Take advantage of any *Employer Match in a 401(k)*. If your company has a 401(k) program with a matching employer contribution, you *must* be utilizing this vehicle. Otherwise you are giving up a 100% rate of return on your money *before* it ever goes into the market. This strategy is critical to building long-term savings so that you can survive any financial crisis.

Step Seven: *Diversification I – Asset Classes*. Your long-term savings should be diversified among multiple asset classes. In simpler terms, you should be investing in stocks of large, medium and small sized companies, along with international companies of various sizes, real estate, and multiple classes of bonds (government and corporate of varying durations). The proportion of these different classes to one another should be determined by your tolerance for risk, which can be ascertained typically using a simple questionnaire. The most common way of accomplishing this type of diversification is through mutual funds, and that is a fine strategy with the least risk to the investor.

Step Eight: *Diversification II – Tax Deferred/Tax Free.* In a rising tax environment like the one we appear to be in, it is imperative that you move some long-term assets into tax-free vehicles. Typically, the average person is saving in only an IRA or a 401(k), which are tax deferred, or they are not utilizing tax favorable investing at all. Consider using a Roth 401(k), if it is offered by your company, and a Roth IRA, if you are eligible for it – as well as other tax-free vehicles, such as Permanent Life Insurance.

AVOIDING THE CRISIS COMPLETELY: With the right amount of planning today, you may be able to avoid a crisis altogether. But even if a crisis arises, proper planning will allow you to withstand it.

Step Nine: Seek professional help – *Utilize Financial Advisers* – Statistics show that those who use financial advisers care more about their families, their assets and their futures. Add to that the advice they are given, and that puts you miles ahead of others.

Step Ten: Create a financial plan that encompasses all of the above and *stick to the financial plan.*

Step Eleven: *Annually review* the plan to determine if there are any needed changes. Your life changes every year, and so your plan should be fluid. Expanding families, different jobs, and new houses all necessitate a review that may involve some changes to your plan. Each of these personal, professional or family changes, without proper review, could increase the likelihood of a crisis that may have been avoidable with proper planning.

Step Twelve: *Budget* – It all starts with *cash flow.* Without a true understanding of your monthly cash flow, it is hard to work within a plan. Look at all sources of after-tax income, and then all monthly expenses, and create a budget that will allow you to address the issues above so that you can survive and even avoid a crisis. Also, try to save 10% of after tax income each month. Then *stick to the budget*!

Twelve Step Program to Use Fitness During Crisis

By Josh Bowen, Physical Fitness Professional

The human body is a weird, dynamic and fascinating thing, all at the same time. Our bodies counteract our stress with hormone production to help alleviate the situation. A smart scientist named Hans Selye defined stress as the "nonspecific response of the body to any demand put on it." In times of crisis, fitness and nutrition can be used to balance out the human body.

During a crisis, the human body will secrete several hormones due to its reaction to the stress. For example, if a person reacts to crisis as a challenge to his or her control of a situation, the body will produce *norepinephrine*, the fight hormone. If a person is in a crisis and feels a loss of control, *epinephrine* will be released. If a person feels a prolonged crisis where they feel a complete loss of control, the body will produce *cortisol*. If this process happens often, as in times of crisis, it can be detrimental to the human body.

So here is how we can use fitness and nutrition as our vehicle to help us during times of turmoil and crisis:

Step One: *Nutrition, Science*: Our hormones have a big impact on our bodies; crisis and stress enhance that. Nutritionally, we eat to survive, but we can also eat to thrive. Excessive cortisol production will cause our bodies to tear down muscle tissue and cause us to store unwanted body fat. It will also suppress our immune systems during times of stress. Not good.

Step Two: *Nutrition, Practical*: Foods shown to reduce cortisol production are eggs, lean beef, sweet potatoes, fruits, and lots of vegetables. Raw, organic vegetables are preferred because of the high amounts of vitamin C, a cortisol reducer and anti-inflammatory.

Step Three: *Resistance Training, Science*: The human body does not know the difference between "good" stress or "bad" stress. So any stress put upon it will cause hormone secretion. Resistance training (lifting weights) is a stress to the body; however, it allows your body to strengthen and grow your muscles and strengthen your bones, which is very important in times of crisis. Also, it will allow you to blow off much-needed steam.

Step Four: *Resistance Training, Practical*: If you are a beginner, start with three to four days of resistance training. Make sure you give your body 48-72 hours between body parts before you hit them again. As you progress, you can start incorporating Tabatas, plyometrics, and cross training into your program. Make sure you get ample rest and nutrition, as this will enable recovery and reduce your stressful situation.

Step Five: *Cardiovascular conditioning, Science*: It is said that the heart is the most important muscle in your body. That is correct, for without your heart, most processes in the body could not take place. The heart transports blood, oxygen, and waste amongst other things. It cannot take heavy stress over a long period of time. Diet, exercise and reduced stress play an enormous part in the heart's health. In times of crisis, the heart takes a pounding due to increased hormone secretion, high blood pressure and increased anxiety.

Step Six: *Cardiovascular Training, Practical*: Strengthen your heart by activity, not just cardio. Cardiovascular training will help increase the amount of blood pumped in a heartbeat, thus making it more efficient. Three to four days of vigorous activity is best. Beware overdoing cardio, which also causes stress to the body. Keep it simple in times of crisis.

Steve Seven: *Holistic Health, Science*: Taking into account more than just practical medicine, holistic health is a huge part of wellbeing during a crisis. Here we will concentrate on herbs that will reduce cortisol production and holistically improve your body, versus turning to practical medicines.

Step Eight: *Holistic Health, Practical*: Black tea, green tea, and ginkgo all have cortisol reducing properties. Implement them into your diet and watch your stress levels and cortisol production decrease.

Step Nine: *Meditation, Science*: As discussed earlier, rest and relaxation play as big a part of crisis control as fitness. Being able to relax and meditate will increase serotonin production to relax the body.

Step Ten: *Meditation, Practical*: Take 15-30 minutes per day and shut out all the distractions, and just let your mind and body relax. If need be, get a massage!

Step Eleven: *Flexibility/Yoga, Science*: Yoga/meditation/massage all have similar outcomes on the brain, allowing you to relax and shut out the world's problems. Becoming more flexible will reduce the amount of muscular stress on your body, thereby helping with the overall stress.

Step Twelve: *Flexibility/Yoga, Practical*: Take a yoga class, or just take time to do some dynamic stretches like lunges or body weight squats – it will do wonders for your flexibility, joints, tissue strength and stress levels.

Twelve Step Program to Survive a Crisis of the Heart – and Find "The One"

By Nancy Slotnick, Founder, Matchmaker Café

Step One: Make your love life a Number One Priority (i.e. if your boss asks you to stay late, consider your dating plans to be as important as if you had a child at home waiting for you.)

Step Two: Spend 15 Hours per week on "the Search." Note: This includes online dating, but don't overdose – three hours daily at the most.

Step Three: Try to have one date per week. If you truly spend 15 hours per week on the Search, then this will come naturally.

Step Four: Clear your plate. Ex-girlfriends/boyfriends or friends with benefits are often deterrents to finding someone new.

Step Five: Smile at strangers.

Step Six: Talk to ten new people per week.

Step Seven: Work your network. Get in touch with Facebook friends you never see. Re-connect with high school acquaintances. Make new wing man/wing woman friends.

Step Eight: Name that tune in fewer notes: If you have a date and you are lukewarm, move on. Don't waste time trying to make yourself like someone.

<u>Step Nine</u>: Get good at rejecting and being rejected. It's par for the course. Every "No" leads you closer to a "Yes."

<u>Step Ten</u>: If you meet someone you like, zero in. Try to date that person exclusively for a month and see how it goes. Dating others at the same time makes it harder to assess your feelings in a vacuum.

<u>Step Eleven</u>: Wait to sleep with the person until you are dating exclusively. Build momentum by seeing each other at least once per week, hopefully more.

<u>Step Twelve</u>: Make yourself vulnerable. At every turn, choose the braver path of admitting interest and putting yourself "out there," even before it is reciprocated. People who are willing to make themselves vulnerable first get more of what they want out of life.

Twelve Step Program for Surviving Crisis in the Academic World

By Ronald J. Granieri, former
Professor, University of Pennsylvania

Academia offers a profession different from many others, first by being one of the few where one begins training not even knowing if there will be a job at the end, while at the same time enmeshing one's work and identity like no other. Being a professor is a job, a lifestyle, a craft, and a calling. It is also a vanishing breed. The once-common traditional path of PhD, then teaching job, then tenure for life at one institution is becoming increasingly rare, as the number of full-time tenure track positions shrinks, and the competition to get and keep those positions gets ever tighter.

After years of essentially ignoring the possibility that many of their students might have to seek employment somewhere other than a college faculty, universities are only now trying to give advice on possible alternatives. But it is not that easy for professors trained according to that old paradigm to offer helpful advice about the new world. Often they say nothing, suggesting that even considering alternatives is a sign that one is not serious about academic life. As a result, graduate students and junior faculty feel especially alone and vulnerable. They face the frightening prospect of never getting officially onto the tenure track, or the possibility of getting pushed off somewhere along the way with no guarantee that one can get back on.

Once exiled from campus, they often have no idea where to turn for advice.

As someone who has been pushed off the tenure track, and who at present has no clear path back onto it, I have spent some time thinking about how one recovers, and offer these twelve steps. I can't say I followed them all as well as one should, but I think they offer a way out of the depressed helplessness that follows academic rejection.

These twelve steps are generally in order, though they do tend to overlap in places. They offer a way for academics facing life off the tenure track to shake that sense of losing their identity and to reclaim their sense of self-worth as they move forward:

Step One: Let go of the pain: This is the simplest thing to say, but often the hardest to do. You have to accept that it hurts to be rejected, but also realize that holding onto the pain does no good. Sooner or later, you have to put it aside. You may not forget it completely for some time, but there is no need to cultivate it either.

Step Two: Remember that a grade is not an evaluation of you as a human being: I often said this to students while returning an assignment, and it is important to remember in your own case as well. The decision by a search committee or a tenure board is an evaluation of your work according to the criteria under which they operated, some of which you might not even completely know. It may well be that you were not right for that post under those criteria, but this is not a referendum on your humanity.

Step Three: Learn from the past, but face the future: Related to the two steps above, you have to accept that you can't re-run the search, or replay everything about it. Did you mess up a question in the interview? Do you wish you had completed that article before the deadline? That may be, and you can learn from those actions. But that learning can only be applied forward. It does no good to dwell on a past that cannot be re-run.

Step Four: Try to separate personal disappointment from your evaluation of the system: I have had a hard time with this. Of course, one can feel like a victim of injustice; it is certainly true that the system needs reforms. But such reforms will or will not happen because people advance them for their own sake. This relates to the step above, a realization that even future changes cannot undo what has been done. You can only overcome the past by working for a better future, not by trying to repeat the past.

Step Five: Pause and reconsider what interested you from the start: As you pivot toward the future, you need to remember why you chose your path of study. To be a professor, sure, but you had to be motivated by more than one vision of employment. What was it about your subject that interested you, that grabbed you? That is the foundation of your new start.

Step Six: Use this opportunity to re-focus on what you really want to do: So you may not be a full-time faculty member after all. What was it about that job that interested you? The teaching? The research? The participation in an academic community? The tweed jackets? There is nothing that says those things are lost to you; you need to consider how to keep them in your life.

Step Seven: Decide which relationships are important to maintain: This starts with the humdrum: those academic journals you subscribed to or organizations you joined, and moves on to the people with whom you used to work. All of those connections may have had their place in your old life, but you need not feel compelled to keep all of them. At the same time, you should not just drift away from your old life. You need to be thoughtful and careful, choosing which connections to maintain and cultivate. Mindfulness is essential.

Step Eight: Take stock of what you have learned, and what you have to offer: Your life up to now had meaning, and even though your life is changing, that meaning has not somehow evaporated. Consider who you are at this moment, building on what you have been – the skills you developed, the experiences that shaped you.

Step Nine: Don't be afraid to start something new: After having focused all your attention on one career path, it can be difficult to imagine alternatives. But your skills and experience can take you in other directions. You need to be practical, of course, but not afraid.

Step Ten: Ask for help: You probably will not be able to think of all the possibilities on your own. Which is why you should not try. Don't retreat into yourself; talk to friends and loved ones. Let them help you, be open to their ideas, and your own will be enriched. When I was at my lowest, my wife offered validation and love, and a good friend and colleague offered me a job that temporarily provided stability, until another friend came along to offer a more permanent job to follow.

Step Eleven: Listen to your actual calling: Here it gets a little scary. After taking the previous steps, you will begin to hear the options out there. Some may be obvious, others unfamiliar. But you need to be open to what you hear, to listen closely. What I am doing now is different from what I thought I would be doing, though there are connections that have made the transition easier.

Step Twelve: Pursue the new path: Now that you see it, all that remains is to get started.

Twelve Step Program to Surviving the Crisis of Freshman Year of College

By Emily Miller, Student, Miami University of Ohio

Step One: Don't pack your entire closet – there most likely won't be enough room for all your clothes.

Step Two: Always have plenty of healthy snacks on hand.

Step Three: Learn how to do laundry before you get to school.

Step Four: Sign up for classes that look interesting and exciting.

Step Five: Go to class.

Step Six: Go to your professor's office hours if you need help.

Step Seven: Go to class.

Step Eight: Don't walk alone at night – make sure you always have a buddy with you.

Step Nine: Don't drink the jungle juice – it's a lot stronger than you think. (So I've been told by my 21-year-old friends, who are of legal drinking age.)

Step Ten: If your mom gets mad at you for your college activities, remind her of what your dad did in college.

<u>Step Eleven</u>: If you don't like your first semester, give it another semester – it gets much better.

<u>Step Twelve</u>: Be safe but have fun: They say these are the best years of your life.

Twelve Step Program to Maintaining Sartorial Splendor and Avoiding Fashion Crisis

By Julie Rath, Men's Image and Style Consultant and Founder of Rath & Co.

Step One: Your tailor is your best friend (look at user-review sites like Yelp and Citysearch to find a good one in your area). He can take boxy off-the-rack clothes and make them look like a custom job.

Step Two: The only time you should wear a button-up shirt untucked is if it's designed to be casual. This means it's cut with a shallow curve across the bottom (unlike the pronounced tails on your dress shirt), and the hem hits between the waistband of your pants and your hip-bone. Otherwise, it looks sloppy and says you don't know how to dress casually.

Step Three: Avoid wearing the same pair of shoes two days in a row. Instead rotate them, and make sure you use shoe trees. You'll double the life of your shoes.

Step Four: Make sure that both the leathers (i.e., shoes and belt) and the metals (i.e., watch face and belt buckle) in your look match in color.

Step Five: Don't let your t-shirt show beneath your dress shirt. Wear an undershirt with a deep v-neck to avoid issues.

Step Six: The best way to clean your dress shirts so they look great and last a long time is to have them laundered and hand-ironed without starch.

Step Seven: Black suits are OK for pallbearers, but they are not appropriate for a business environment.

Step Eight: Don't wear a backpack with a suit or sport coat. It's terrible for the shoulders of your jacket, not to mention that the look isn't cohesive.

Step Nine: Putting all of your personal effects in your pockets adds bulk and will stretch out your clothing. Better to get an everyday carryall in which you can comfortably place all of your daily necessities.

Step Ten: Avoid overly gelled hair. Use a cream or wax-based product instead to avoid that "wet" look.

Step Eleven: Depart the 90's: Square-toed shoes are a must-miss.

Step Twelve: Avoid hybrid sneaker-shoes. It's a sneaker OR a shoe. Not both.

Twelve Step Program for Social Media Crisis Management

By Courtney Spritzer and Stephanie Abrams, Co-Founders, SOCIALFLY

Social media networks such as Facebook and Twitter have made public access to your opinion and the opinions of others easier than it has ever been. These vehicles allow one to share thoughts, through publicly posted comments, that can easily be seen by *all* in *real-time*. However, these public forums can be both a blessing and a burden. Your approach to managing a crisis should be well thought out and carefully considered; including social media in this strategy is paramount:

Step One: Learn what's out there: Facebook, Twitter, Pinterest, Instagram, LinkedIn. The list of social media vehicles continues to grow. Some, such as MySpace, fade over time. However, the principles they are based on do not. Social networks simply find a way to evolve and thrive.

Step Two: Understand the magnitude of social media: It's enormous. There are over 141 million Twitter users in the U.S. alone, and its popularity abroad is skyrocketing. Facebook reaches an even broader audience, now boasting over one billion users. This growth makes the potential reach these social media platforms offer ideal for sharing political opinion. According to a statement released by Twitter, this potential was realized this past 2012 election, with a record 31.7 million political related tweets published.[77]   As Election Day 2012 has been declared the most tweeted about event in U.S. political history to date, the ability of social media to influence political process was crystallized. As it relates to handling crisis, one now has the means to extinguish an ember of controversy before it sparks a firestorm.

Step Three: Learn the benefits: There are a wealth of advantages for social media crisis management. The ability to directly see what people are saying about you and/or discover a blossoming scandal is political gold. When even just a hint of a scandal merges, you can expect it to break on Twitter first. While the ease of access to Twitter is invaluable in allowing you to stay on top of public opinion, it also has another treasured side effect – reverberation. The comments, likes, and posts shared by one user ripple through their entire online network of friends and family. Your followers and fans are not the only ones seeing and/or sharing your message. It is *everyone* they associate with. This reach is powerful. Sharing the correct message by these means is direct, efficient, and impactful.

Step Four: Understand how social media are a two-way street: The public nature of this particular platform allows you to directly search for what is currently being said about a desired topic. The days of sweating it out, waiting for the latest public opinion poll from traditional media avenues are over. The live forums social media sites provide circulate the thoughts and feelings of hundreds of millions across the web everyday. If these public comments are weighed and evaluated properly, it is now possible to tailor an informed crisis strategy, which allows you to directly target and address the most common public misconceptions of your issue.

Step Five: Follow the evolving blueprint: With social media still rapidly evolving, the blueprint of how to effectively use these platforms to manage political crisis is still being written. While former Congressman Anthony Weiner and others have shown the world how social media can cause direct harm to a politician, examples of the contrary are still gestating. However, there is still a set of core principles to follow and think about while including social media in your plan.

Step Six: Develop a social media strategy: Social media doesn't just speak public opinion; it shouts it from the mountaintops. Having easy, direct access to public sentiment provides powerful knowledge. However, this knowledge is useless if not properly used to facilitate a strategy bent on successfully overcoming political crisis.

Step Seven: Learn your audience. What are people posting? How is their network responding? What are the key themes in their debates? What are the most common misconceptions?

Step Eight: Target certain detractors to respond to: Avoid engaging in debate with hostile commenters. With access available to all 24/7, responding to all isn't realistic. It is okay to stay silent. Don't open the floodgates of unwanted opinions and ignorant rants. Remember, many beyond the user with whom you are interacting will see these interactions.

Step Nine: Keep your message friendly, polite, and concise. Stay professional, classy, and consistent. Discretion and restraint are mandatory. We shouldn't have to warn you about posting shirtless pictures. Stay human. Not only can it show humility, it can teach it. Besides, without Facebook and Twitter, how else are you going to know how "#moronic," "#inept," and "#ineffectual" you really are...if stated that kindly!

Step Ten: Don't be afraid to be playful. If we look to the positive potential of this ability to interact with the public, we see someone like Senator Marco Rubio turning a gaffe into a $100K online/social media based fundraiser. Rubio was attacked by the media about his decision to drink from a water bottle in the middle of his televised response to President Barack Obama's State of Union address. He used this media uproar to his advantage by posting pictures of his branded water bottle online and poking fun at the situation. He showed he was human, and handled it with humility, while helping quiet the chatter.[78]

<u>Step Eleven</u>: Listen to your audience and choose when to respond and when to keep radio silence. You are reaching and hearing from many. So even if you choose not to respond through these networks, you can use the data compiled when preparing for speech or debate. Heck, might as well tailor traditional P.R. releases with this data too.

<u>Step Twelve</u>: Consult and collaborate with a professional adviser: If you have a little money to invest, a social media adviser can be an invaluable resource in charting a course of social media crisis management. Feel free to contact us for ideas![79]

Twelve Step Program to Surviving Friendship Crises in High School

By Abby Miller, Student, Lafayette High School

Step One: Always arm yourself with a package of gum. Not only is good smelling breath an admirable quality, but you'll also find that everyone suddenly wants to be your friend when they see you have gum.

Step Two: Instead of talking about yourself, listen to other people's problems. Teenagers are very self-obsessed and love to talk about themselves, so if you can tune someone out while also maintaining an engaged expression, you'll be thought of as a great friend.

Step Three: Make fun of your teachers behind their backs. A common enemy always brings people together.

Step Four: Join lots of clubs. It doesn't matter if you don't know what the club is even for. Odds are, there will be free food, and people easily bond over free doughnuts.

Step Five: Put lots of cool hipster music on your iPod even if you don't care for it. The moment someone sees you listen to his or her favorite obscure band, you will gain immediate street cred.

Step Six: Offer to give people rides. Most high schoolers don't own their own cars, and gas is too expensive for teens that don't work part time in a grease bucket or watching screaming children. But if you're willing to sacrifice a few extra bucks, a friendship can be greatly strengthened.

Step Steven: Get Instagram, Facebook, and Twitter. All three are needed to keep up on the appropriate gossip of high school drama. The last thing you want to be is the clueless person bugging everyone with questions about happenings on social media.

Step Eight: Watch lots of popular T.V. shows. Snooki who? You better be prepared to talk about her and her contemporaries at school the next day, or else you'll be left out of the lunchtime conversation.

Step Nine: Join a sports team. Not good at sports? That's OK! There are always intramural or club teams that mostly consist of laughing at your failures and goofing off; prime time for making new friends.

Step Ten: Don't brag. The last thing people want to hear is how you got a perfect score on the chemistry test while they completely bombed it. You don't want the reputation of being snooty and insensitive.

Step Eleven: Don't be afraid to be a little weird. Everyone is a little weird inside and loves to be around weird people so they can act on their weirdness.

Step Twelve: Be nice! If anything, you want to come out of high school being known as a good person. A bland but kind reputation is better than one of a bratty prima donna or a cold-hearted scorpion.

Twelve Step Program to Surviving a Travel Crisis

By Matt and Erica Chua, Proprietors of LivingIF

Traveling is stressful. Whether you find yourself in San Francisco or Somalia, anxiety is an ever-present feeling because the unknown plays to our worst fears. While the real dangers may be the same, being in a place we don't know makes us worry. Don't fret though, as long as you have access to funds and a phone you can get home...here's how to prepare, avoid and deal with a travel crisis:

PREPARING FOR CRISIS*:*

<u>Step One:</u> *Have two ATM and credit cards, issued by different banks.* If one gets lost, stolen or cut-off, the other should still be able to get you cash.

<u>Step Two:</u> *Have a Skype account with $10 in credit.* Setting an account up in a time of need will make a bad situation even worse, but having an account will save a lot of headache. Being able to make calls from wi-fi-equipped phones, laptops and virtually all Internet cafes for pennies will allow you to sort basically anything out for under $10. That same $10 won't go far on a hotel phone.

<u>Step Three</u>*: Save your bank's emergency contact numbers in your Skype contacts.* If you need to make a call, have the emergency

numbers where you need to call them from: Skype.

<u>Step Four:</u> *Hide $100 USD somewhere in a bag you leave at your hotel.* Stuff this somewhere that isn't visible and surrounded by worthless things (Band Aids?) to make sure you have a little cash if everything else is lost.

AVOIDING CRISIS:

<u>Step Five:</u> *Carry only what you need while sightseeing.* The more things you have, the more you have to pay attention to, the more likely you'll present thieves opportunities to relieve you of important things. Have one small bag, necessary clothing, your camera and anything you *need*.

<u>Step Six</u>: *If you get spilled on, don't stop...start moving.* This is a global pickpocket scheme: Spray something on someone, come up to call attention to it, start helping clean it...all the while pickpocketing you. Distraction is the name of the game, when you're wondering how you got that on yourself, the helpful locals are helping themselves to your possessions.

<u>Step Seven</u>: *Never let people follow you closely.* If you're in an open area, and someone is walking close behind, assume they are trying to get something from you. While there is no avoiding the crowds in a Tokyo subway, on open sidewalks, make sure you're an arms-length away from everyone. Be suspect of anyone, especially children, coming within your "circle of trust".

<u>Step Eight:</u> *Keep zippers at the bottom, ideally clipped together.* Zippers meeting at the center of your bag are an invitation for a hand to reach in. Zippers put near the bottom of the bag force would-be thieves to exert more effort and probably arouse your suspicion. It's even better if you can clip the zippers in a way that doesn't allow them to be separated easily.

RESPONDING TO CRISIS:

<u>Step Nine:</u> *Don't panic, it's not the end of the world.* Worse things have happened, probably even in the city you are visiting.

<u>Step Ten:</u> *Identify everything you lost.* This will make sure you have everything for insurance.

<u>Step Eleven:</u> *Call your banks (if necessary).* If you will need money in the near-term, and they are the only option, see if they will let you leave an account open for a few hours to get you set up. In your worst moments, they really want to help, so be patient; it's not their fault after all, and they'll help you out.

<u>Step Twelve:</u> *Don't let it ruin your trip.* Enjoy your trip as much as you can, because you're probably never going back there!

      The reality is that while traveling, robberies are the most common crime. Almost every developed or touristed country has less violent crimes than the U.S. What travelers need to fear is making themselves victims of opportunity. Wandering the streets distracted, guidebook-in-hand, makes you a likely mark. While taking in the sights, be aware of your surroundings, and the thieves will seek out easier prey. If you do get robbed, remember that it could happen anywhere, in your hometown and while traveling in places you love; but it's not the whole city or every citizen, only a few bad apples...don't let them spoil your trip.

Endnotes

1 "Ron Ziegler, Press Secretary to Nixon, is Dead at 63," *New York Times*, February 11, 2003.
2 "The Elusive Front-Runner; GARY HART," *The New York Times*, May 3, 1987.
3 *Don't Shoot the Albatross! Nautical Myths and Superstitions*, Jonathan Evers, 2011.
4 "Gore, Babbitt Say They've Tried Pot," *The Victoria Advocate*, Nov 7, 1987.
5 "Whole Foods CEO's anonymous online life," *NBC News*, June 14, 2007.
6 "Woods wins UK court ban against nude, sex photos," *Reuters*, December 11, 2009.
7 "Speaker candidate Simpson lashes out at anonymous critics," *American-Statesman*, December 20, 2012.
8 "Ford Exec Blasts Oracle On Social Media For Anonymous Campaign Trashing Competitors," *Silicon Beat*, http://www.siliconbeat.com/2012/10/09/ford-exec-blasts-oracle-on-social-media-for-anonymous-campaign-trashing-competitors/.
9 "Grayson Wants Critic Jailed for Claiming to be His Constituent," *Fox News*, http://www.foxnews.com/politics/2009/12/22/grayson-wants-critic-jailed-claiming-constituent/
10 "Law Professor (?!?) Claims Copyright Infringement Because Blog Uses Faculty Photo In Blog Post," *Law Dirt*, http://www.techdirt.com/articles/20091104/0139026792.shtml
11 "When Authors Attack," *The Guardian*, December 22, 2008.
12 See, http://www.thestreisandeffect.com for examples of this phenomenon, several of which were excerpted above.
13 Presidential Papers of John F. Kennedy, 139 - The President's News Conference, April 21, 1961.
14 "RFK's Fourth Child Eased the Pain of His Father's Death with Drugs and Drink, But the Prescription Proved Tragically Fatal," *People*, May 14, 1984.
15 "How I Avoided Suicide," Douglas Bloch, http://www.healingfromdepression.com/how-i-avoided-suicide.htm
16 *The Complete Stories*, Flannery O'Connor, 1971.
17 *Cannery Row*, John Steinbeck, 1993.
18 See, http://health.groups.yahoo.com/group/AAHistoryLovers/message/182
19 *Iron John: A Book About Men*, Robert Bly, 2004.
20 *Switch*, Chip Heath and Dan Heath, 2009.
21 "Tyler Hamilton: 'Now the truth about doping will come out,'" *The Guardian*, September 24, 2012.

[22] *Charlie Wilson's War: The Extraordinary Story of How the Wildest Man in Congress and a Rogue CIA Agent Changed the History of Our Times*, George Crile, 2007.

[23] "New York's Charles Rangel faces 13 Ethics Charges," *USA Today*, July 30, 2010.

[24] "Transcript: Rep. Charles Rangel's Remarks on Controversial Academic Center," *CQ Transcripts Wire*, Thursday, July 17, 2008.

[25] "The Anthony Weiner scandal: How it all went wrong," *Los Angeles Times*, June 16, 2011.

[26] "Costa Concordia wreck leaves hostile PR wake for Carnival Cruise Lines," *The Miami Herald*, January 24, 2012.

[27] "Boss of Carnival cruise ship adds insult to misery by going to basketball game as 4,000 suffer aboard 'stinking stricken ship' with urine-soaked carpets and sewage in cabins," *Daily Mail*, May 13, 2012.

[28] "Breakthrough in cold case: FBI probe 'incriminating video' of guests on cruise ship where groom fell overboard to his death on honeymoon seven years ago," *Daily Mail*, May 28, 2012.

[29] http://www.royalcaribbeanblog.com/

[30] CNN, "Larry King Live," January 10, 2006.

[31] *Crisis Tales: Five Rules for Coping with Crises in Business, Politics, and Life*, Lanny Davis, 2013.

[32] "Levy on immigrant killing: Just a one-day story!!!," *Newsday*, November 11, 2008.

[33] "Gov. Christie praises Obama's response to Hurricane Sandy as 'outstanding,'" *The Hill*, October 30, 2012.

[34] "LIPA Exec Resigns Amid Rising Fury Over Sandy Outages," *NBC New York*, November 14, 2012.

[35] "Gov. Cuomo's focus on Hurricane Sandy boosts his national profile," *New York Daily News*, November 20, 2012.

[36] "Steve Levy response to grand jury ethics report," *Newsday*, April 19, 2012.

[37] http://www.centerforcosteffectivegovernment.org/

[38] "In Endorsements, No Athlete Is a Sure Thing," *New York Times*, August 1, 2007.

[39] "Vick, Eagles agree to 2-year deal," *ESPN.com*, August 14, 2009.

[40] Humane Society Web site: http://www.humanesociety.org/issues/dogfighting/qa/vick_faq.html

[41] "Michael Vick Now Has A Dog Somehow," *Sports Grid*, October 6, 2012.

[42] "Hugh Grant on prostitute charge," *The Telegraph*, June 28, 1995.

[43] "Spin cycle: Hugh Grant finds 'honesty' best policy," *CNN*, July 17, 1995.

[44] "The Anthony Weiner scandal: How it all went wrong," *Los Angeles Times*, June 16, 2011.

[45] "Ex-Atlanta Mayor Guilty of Tax Evasion," *Associated Press*, March 11, 2006.

[46] "Bush calls Katrina photo 'huge mistake'," *CNN*, November 6, 2010.

47 "Hurricane Katrina Left a Mark on George W. Bush's Presidency," *US News & World Report*, December 11, 2008.

48 "In superstorm Sandy, Gov. Chris Christie praises Obama's crisis leadership," *Washington Post*, October 30, 2012.

49 "Crisis triggered brilliant PR response," *Chicago Sun-Times*, Dec. 4, 2002.

50 "Exxon's Public-Relations Problem," *The New York Times*, April 21, 1989.

51 "Wallflower at the Web Party," *The New York Times*, October 15, 2006.

52 "From Facebook, answering privacy concerns with new settings," *Washington Post*, May 24, 2010.

53 See, http://www.nolabels.org/work

54 "Obama to take pay cut to draw attention to plight of federal workers facing furloughs," *Washington Post*, April 3, 2013.

55 "How Jerry Brown Beat Meg Whitman in California," *CBS News*, November 3, 2010.

56 *The Audacity of Hope: Thoughts on Reclaiming the American Dream*, Barack Obama, 2008.

57 "Lazio Calls Debate Criticism 'Sexist,'" *ABC News*, September 20, 2002.

58 "Top 10 Obama Backlash Moments," *Time*, January 1, 2009.

59 "Obama, Clinton pressed on 2016 in joint interview," *Politico*, January 27, 2013.

60 See, http://www.projectnewamerica.com

61 See, http://www.goodreads.com/quotes/1487-the-chinese-use-two-brush-strokes-to-write-the-word?auto_login_attempted=true

62 See, http://staceykingquotes.wordpress.com/

63 "Reagan's Hospital One-Liners Inspired by Hollywood," *US News & World Report*, August 11, 2011.

64 "What changed after the Reagan shooting," *CNN*, March 30, 2011.

65 "When Ronald Reagan Blew a Presidential Debate and Dropped Seven Points in the Polls," *Slate*, October 10, 2012.

66 "Presidential Debates Explainer," *CNN*, October 3, 2012.

67 "Reagan jokes about bombing Russia, August 11, 1984," *Politico*, August 11, 2010.

68 "'Winter in Scotland': How Ashley Judd Will Force the Media to Develop a Sense of Humor," *Huffington Post*, March 12, 2013.

69 "Congress somewhere below cockroaches, traffic jams, and Nickelback in Americans' esteem," *Public Policy Polling*, January 8, 2013.

70 "Bill Clinton's Running Habit: A Secret Service Nightmare," *US News & World Report*, February 29, 2012.

71 "Blair book speculates on Clinton affair," *Politico*, September 3, 2010.

72 "Presidential Job Approval: Bill Clinton's High Ratings in the Midst of Crisis, 1998," *Gallup*, June 4, 1999.

73 "The Pine Tar Incident," *Time*, September 25, 2012.

74 See, http://joeposnanski.blogspot.com/2012/11/musial-redux.html

75 See, http://www.sportsonearth.com/article/41045162

[76] http://www.lisamillerbeautifulday.com/
[77] See, http://www.mediabistro.com/alltwitter/twitter-stats_b32050
[78] "Rubio PAC Offering 'Marco Rubio Water Bottle,'" *ABC News*, February 13, 2013.
[79] http://socialflyny.com/